OFFICIAL

FORTNITE

THE ULTIMATE LOCKER

First published in the UK in 2020 by WILDFIRE an imprint of HEADLINE PUBLISHING GROUP

Cataloguing in Publication Data is available from the British Library

Paperback 978 14722 7243 0

Design by Amazing 15

All images © Epic Games, Inc.

Printed and bound in Italy by L.E.G.O. S.p.A.

Every effort has been made to fulfil requirements with regard to reproducing copyright material. The
author and publisher will be glad to rectify any omissions at the earliest opportunity.

Headline's policy is to use papers that are natural, renewable and recyclable products and made
from wood grown in sustainable forests. The logging and manufacturing processes are expected to
conform to the environmental regulations of the country of origin.

HEADLINE PUBLISHING GROUP
An Hachette UK Company
Carmelite House
50 Victoria Embankment
London, EC4 0DZ
www.headline.co.uk www.hachette.co.uk

Little, Brown and Company
Hachette Book Group
1290 Avenue of the Americas, New York, NY 10104
Visit us at LBYR.com

www.epicgames.com

First Edition: May 2020

First U.S. Edition: June 2020

Little, Brown and Company is a division of Hachette Book Group, Inc.

The Little, Brown name and logo are trademarks of Hachette Book Group, Inc.

The publisher is not responsible for websites (or their content) that are not owned by the publisher.

ISBNs: 978-0-316-43002-9 (pbk), 978-0-316-42998-6 (ebook), 978-0-316-42999-3 (ebook), 978-0-316-43000-5 (ebook)

U.S. edition printed in the United States of America

All images © Epic Games, Inc.

CW
UK Paperback: 10 9 8 7 6 5 4 3 2 1
U.S. Paperback: 10 9 8 7 6 5 4 3 2 1

OFFICIAL
FORTNITE
THE ULTIMATE LOCKER

WILDFIRE

CONTENTS

WELCOME TO THE ULTIMATE LOCKER...

where you can find just about every Outfit, Back Bling, Pet, Harvesting Tool, Glider and Umbrella, Contrail, and Emote from Fortnite Seasons 1 to X—all in one volume.

Covering everything from Aerial Assault Trooper to Zorgoton, this book is divided by season so it's easy to see how Fortnite has grown since it launched in July 2017. Check out the set information to find out which items belong together and tick off the ones you own. Don't know your Vulture from your Vendetta? Here you can brush up on your knowledge of the rarest and most coveted Fortnite fan favorites!

Featuring over 1,600 illustrations, along with dozens of fun facts, this book is the ULTIMATE visual encyclopedia of Fortnite.

30 skins
2 back blings
10 harvesting tools
13 gliders
1 emote
0 contrails

SEASON 1

AERIAL ASSAULT TROOPER
RARITY: RARE

ASSAULT TROOPER
RARITY: UNCOMMON

BRAWLER
RARITY: RARE

COMMANDO
RARITY: UNCOMMON

DESPERADO
RARITY: RARE

FIRST STRIKE SPECIALIST
RARITY: RARE

GHOUL TROOPER
RARITY: EPIC

INFILTRATOR
RARITY: RARE

MUNITIONS EXPERT
RARITY: RARE

PATHFINDER
RARITY: UNCOMMON

RANGER
RARITY: UNCOMMON

RECON EXPERT
RARITY: RARE

RECON SCOUT
RARITY: RARE

RECON SPECIALIST
RARITY: RARE

RECRUIT (BANSHEE)
RARITY: COMMON

RECRUIT (HAWK)
RARITY: COMMON

RECRUIT (HEADHUNTER)
RARITY: COMMON

RECRUIT (JONESY)
RARITY: COMMON

RECRUIT (RAMIREZ)
RARITY: COMMON

RECRUIT (RENEGADE)
RARITY: COMMON

RECRUIT (SPITFIRE)
RARITY: COMMON

RECRUIT (WILDCAT)
RARITY: COMMON

RENEGADE
RARITY: UNCOMMON

RENEGADE RAIDER
RARITY: RARE
SET: STORM SCAVENGER

SCOUT
RARITY: UNCOMMON

SKULL TROOPER
RARITY: EPIC
SET: SKULL SQUAD

SPECIAL FORCES
RARITY: RARE

SURVIVAL SPECIALIST
RARITY: RARE

TRACKER
RARITY: UNCOMMON

TROOPER
RARITY: UNCOMMON

ORTNITE FACTS
CON EXPERT, RENEGADE RAIDER,
D AERIAL ASSAULT TROOPER ARE
NSIDERED AMONG THE RAREST
TFITS IN FORTNITE.

17

FORTNITE FACTS

THE BONE-CRUNCHING SKULL TROOPER COMPLETELY DISAPPEARED FROM THE ITEM SHOP AFTER ITS INITIAL RELEASE AND DID NOT REAPPEAR UNTIL SEASON 8.

BRITE BAG
RARITY: EPIC
SET: SUNSHINE & RAINBOWS

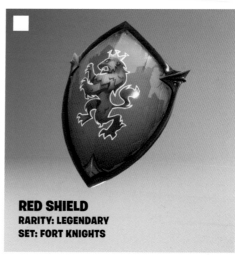

RED SHIELD
RARITY: LEGENDARY
SET: FORT KNIGHTS

FORTNITE FACTS

BACK BLING WASN'T A FEATURE OF FORTNITE UNTIL SEASON 2, BUT BRITE BAG AND RED SHIELD CAME OUT THE DAY BEFORE THE SEASON 2 LAUNCH, SO TECHNICALLY THEY FALL INTO THE FIRST SEASON.

BATSICKLE
RARITY: RARE

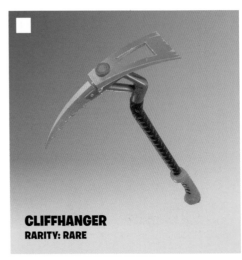

CLIFFHANGER
RARITY: RARE

CLOSE SHAVE
RARITY: RARE

DEATH VALLEY
RARITY: EPIC

DEFAULT
RARITY: COMMON

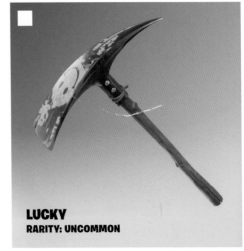

LUCKY
RARITY: UNCOMMON

PINK FLAMINGO
RARITY: EPIC

RAIDER'S REVENGE
RARITY: EPIC

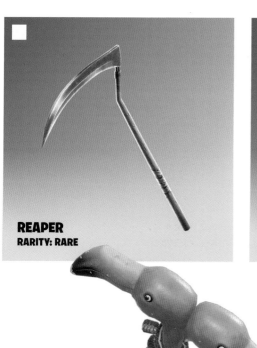

REAPER
RARITY: RARE

SPIKY
RARITY: RARE

FORTNITE FACTS
THE DISTINCTIVE PINK FLAMINGO IS MADE UP OF TWO LAWN-DECORATION FLAMINGO HEADS, A LENGTH OF GREEN HOSE, AND A SHOVEL HANDLE. BECAUSE, WHY NOT?

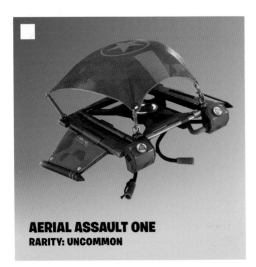

AERIAL ASSAULT ONE
RARITY: UNCOMMON

GLIDER
RARITY: COMMON

HOT ROD
RARITY: UNCOMMON

MAKO
RARITY: UNCOMMON

MODERN
RARITY: UNCOMMON

PETUNIA
RARITY: UNCOMMON

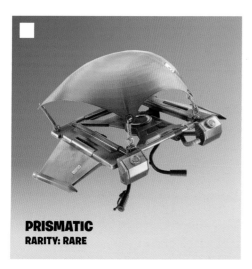

PRISMATIC
RARITY: RARE

RAPTOR
RARITY: UNCOMMON

ROADTRIP
RARITY: UNCOMMON

STEALTH
RARITY: UNCOMMON
SET: STEALTH SYNDICATE

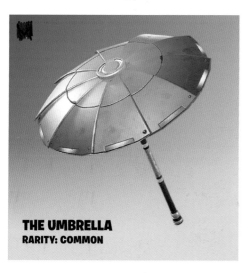

THE UMBRELLA
RARITY: COMMON

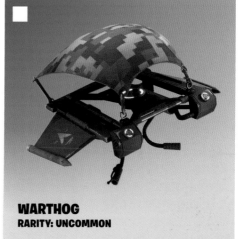

WARTHOG
RARITY: UNCOMMON

WASP
RARITY: UNCOMMON

FORTNITE FACTS

**UMBRELLAS ARE A SPECIAL SUB-CATEGORY OF UNLOCKABLE
GLIDERS THAT CAN ONLY BE OBTAINED IF YOU WIN A VICTORY
ROYALE. EACH SEASON FEATURES ITS OWN DISTINCTIVE
UMBRELLA AND IF YOU WIN A MATCH DURING THAT SEASON,
IT'S YOURS TO USE WHENEVER YOU WANT.**

DANCE MOVES
RARITY: COMMON

FORTNITE FACTS
DANCE MOVES IS THE ONLY COMMON EMOTE IN
FORTNITE, GIVEN TO EVERY PLAYER IN BATTLE
ROYALE, AND IS ONE OF THE FEW EMOTES TO HAVE
MULTIPLE ACCOMPANYING MUSIC TRACKS.

43 skins
10 back bling
14 harvesh to
15 glidess
18 emb
0 contra

SEASON 2

ABSOLUTE ZERO
RARITY: RARE
SET: ARCTIC COMMAND

ALPINE ACE
RARITY: EPIC
SET: WINTER SKI

ALPINE ACE (CAN)
RARITY: EPIC
SET: WINTER SKI

ALPINE ACE (CHN)
RARITY: EPIC
SET: WINTER SKI

ALPINE ACE (FRA)
RARITY: EPIC
SET: WINTER SKI

ALPINE ACE (GBR)
RARITY: EPIC
SET: WINTER SKI

ALPINE ACE (GER)
RARITY: EPIC
SET: WINTER SKI

ALPINE ACE (KOR)
RARITY: EPIC
SET: WINTER SKI

ALPINE ACE (USA)
RARITY: EPIC
SET: WINTER SKI SET

ARCTIC ASSASSIN
RARITY: RARE
SET: ARCTIC COMMAND

BLACK KNIGHT
RARITY: LEGENDARY
SET: FORT KNIGHTS

BLUE SQUIRE
RARITY: RARE
SET: FORT KNIGHTS

BLUE TEAM LEADER
RARITY: RARE

BRITE BOMBER
RARITY: RARE
SET: SUNSHINE & RAINBOWS

CIRCUIT BREAKER
RARITY: RARE
SET: OVERCLOCKED

CODENAME E.L.F.
RARITY: RARE
SET: POLAR LEGENDS

CRACKSHOT
RARITY: LEGENDARY
SET: NUTCRACKER

DEVASTATOR
RARITY: UNCOMMON
SET: STORM FUSION

DOMINATOR
RARITY: UNCOMMON
SET: STORM FUSION

FUNK OPS
RARITY: EPIC
SET: FORTNITE FEVER

GINGER GUNNER
RARITY: EPIC
SET: GINGERBREAD

HYPERION
RARITY: RARE
SET: HYPER

LOVE RANGER
RARITY: LEGENDARY
SET: ROYALE HEARTS

MERRY MARAUDER
RARITY: EPIC
SET: GINGERBREAD

SEASON 2 OUTFITS

MOGUL MASTER
RARITY: EPIC
SET: WINTER SKI

MOGUL MASTER (CAN)
RARITY: EPIC
SET: WINTER SKI

MOGUL MASTER (CHN)
RARITY: EPIC
SET: WINTER SKI

MOGUL MASTER (FRA)
RARITY: EPIC
SET: WINTER SKI

MOGUL MASTER (GBR)
RARITY: EPIC
SET: WINTER SKI

MOGUL MASTER (GER)
RARITY: EPIC
SET: WINTER SKI

MOGUL MASTER (KOR)
RARITY: EPIC
SET: WINTER SKI

MOGUL MASTER (USA)
RARITY: EPIC
SET: WINTER SKI

NOG OPS
RARITY: UNCOMMON

RAPTOR
RARITY: LEGENDARY

RED KNIGHT
RARITY: LEGENDARY
SET: FORT KNIGHTS

RED-NOSED RAIDER
RARITY: RARE

ROYALE KNIGHT
RARITY: RARE
SET: FORT KNIGHTS

SHADOW OPS
RARITY: EPIC
SET: STEALTH SYNDICATE

SNORKEL OPS
RARITY: RARE

SPARKLE SPECIALIST
RARITY: EPIC
SET: FORTNITE FEVER

TACTICS OFFICER
RARITY: UNCOMMON

WUKONG
RARITY: LEGENDARY
SET: WUKONG

YULETIDE RANGER
RARITY: UNCOMMON

ALPINE ACCESSORIES
RARITY: EPIC
SET: WINTER SKI

BLACK SHIELD
RARITY: LEGENDARY
SET: FORT KNIGHTS

CUDDLE BOW
RARITY: LEGENDARY
SET: ROYALE HEARTS

LOVE WINGS
RARITY: LEGENDARY
SET: ROYALE HEARTS

MOGUL SKI BAG
RARITY: EPIC
SET: WINTER SKI

PROSPECT
RARITY: EPIC

RAPTOR SATCHEL
RARITY: LEGENDARY

ROYALE FLAGS
RARITY: LEGENDARY
SET: WUKONG

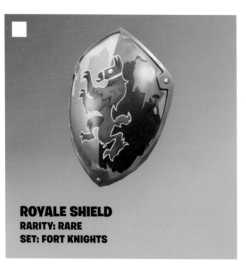

ROYALE SHIELD
RARITY: RARE
SET: FORT KNIGHTS

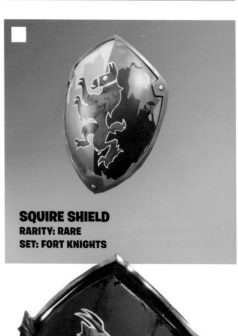

SQUIRE SHIELD
RARITY: RARE
SET: FORT KNIGHTS

FORTNITE FACTS
REFLECTING THE MEDIEVAL THEME, THREE
MORE SHIELDS JOINED RED SHIELD IN
THE FORT KNIGHTS SET THIS SEASON.
IN SEASON X, A FIFTH WAS ADDED: THE
LEGENDARY DRAGONCREST.

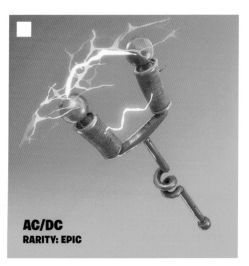

AC/DC
RARITY: EPIC

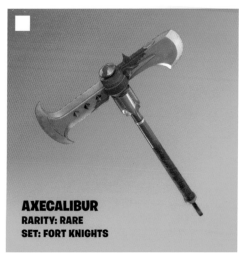

AXECALIBUR
RARITY: RARE
SET: FORT KNIGHTS

BOTTOM FEEDER
RARITY: EPIC

CANDY AXE
RARITY: EPIC

CHOMP JR.
RARITY: EPIC
SET: CHOMP

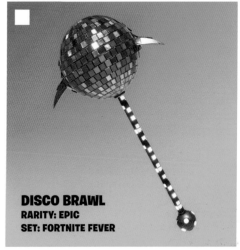

DISCO BRAWL
RARITY: EPIC
SET: FORTNITE FEVER

DRAGON AXE
RARITY: RARE

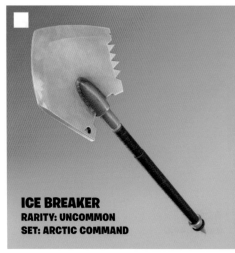

ICE BREAKER
RARITY: UNCOMMON
SET: ARCTIC COMMAND

PARTY ANIMAL
RARITY: EPIC
SET: SLURP SQUAD

PLUNJA
RARITY: RARE

PULSE AXE
RARITY: RARE
SET: STORM FUSION

SKI BOOT
RARITY: RARE
SET: WINTER SKI

TAT AXE
RARITY: RARE
SET: ROYALE HEARTS

YOU SHOULDN'T HAVE!
RARITY: UNCOMMON

FORTNITE FACTS

TAT AXE IS PART OF THE EVER-GROWING ROYALE HEARTS SET, WHICH IN CHAPTER 1 INTRODUCED US TO SUCH OUTFITS AS CUDDLE TEAM LEADER, LOVE RANGER, FALLEN LOVE RANGER, HEARTBREAKER, AND STONEHEART, AS WELL AS TWO GLIDERS: HEARTSPAN AND BEAR FORCE ONE.

BEAR FORCE ONE
RARITY: EPIC
SET: ROYALE HEARTS

BLUE STREAK
RARITY: RARE

CLOUD STRIKE
RARITY: EPIC

COZY COASTER
RARITY: RARE

FIGHTER KITE
RARITY: UNCOMMON

GET DOWN!
RARITY: EPIC
SET: FORTNITE FEVER

GUM DROP
RARITY: RARE

HALF SHELL
RARITY: RARE

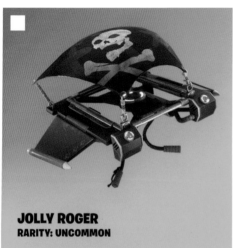

JOLLY ROGER
RARITY: UNCOMMON

ROYALE X
RARITY: UNCOMMON
SET: STORM FUSION

SIR GLIDER THE BRAVE
RARITY: UNCOMMON
SET: FORT KNIGHTS

SNOW SQUALL
RARITY: UNCOMMON
SET: ARCTIC COMMAND

SNOWFLAKE
RARITY: COMMON

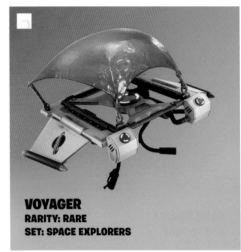

VOYAGER
RARITY: RARE
SET: SPACE EXPLORERS

ZEPHYR
RARITY: RARE

FORTNITE FACTS
BLUE STREAK FEATURED IN THE
FIRST PLAYSTATION PLUS
CELEBRATION PACK, ALONG WITH
THE BLUE TEAM LEADER OUTFIT.

DAB
RARITY: RARE

ELECTRO SHUFFLE
RARITY: EPIC

FINGER GUNS
RARITY: UNCOMMON

FLAPPER
RARITY: RARE

FLOSS
RARITY: RARE

FRESH
RARITY: EPIC

GUN SHOW
RARITY: UNCOMMON

KISS KISS
RARITY: RARE
SET: ROYALE HEARTS

PONY UP
RARITY: RARE

PURE SALT
RARITY: RARE

RIDE THE PONY
RARITY: RARE

SLOW CLAP
RARITY: UNCOMMON

THE WORM
RARITY: RARE

TRUE LOVE
RARITY: UNCOMMON
SET: ROYALE HEARTS

WAVE
RARITY: UNCOMMON

FORTNITE FACTS

KISS KISS AND TRUE LOVE WERE THE FIRST EMOTES TO BE PART OF A SET: ROYALE HEARTS.

36 skins
17 back bli...
17 pick ax...
18 gliders
5 contrails
23 emotes

SEASON 3

BATTLE HOUND
RARITY: LEGENDARY
SET: LAOCH

BRILLIANT STRIKER
RARITY: RARE

BRITE GUNNER
RARITY: EPIC
SET: SUNSHINE & RAINBOWS

BURNOUT
RARITY: EPIC
SET: RPM

CIPHER
RARITY: RARE
SET: OVERCLOCKED

CRIMSON SCOUT
RARITY: UNCOMMON

CUDDLE TEAM LEADER
RARITY: LEGENDARY
SET: ROYALE HEARTS

DARK VANGUARD
RARITY: LEGENDARY
SET: SPACE EXPLORERS

DARK VOYAGER
RARITY: LEGENDARY
SET: SPACE EXPLORERS

DAZZLE
RARITY: RARE
SET: HYPER

ELITE AGENT
RARITY: EPIC
SET: BLACK VECTOR

HAVOC
RARITY: LEGENDARY

HIGHLAND WARRIOR
RARITY: EPIC
SET: LAOCH

HIGHRISE ASSAULT TROOPER
RARITY: UNCOMMON

JUNGLE SCOUT
RARITY: UNCOMMON

LEVIATHAN
RARITY: LEGENDARY
SET: SPACE EXPLORERS

MIDNIGHT OPS
RARITY: RARE
SET: STEALTH SYNDICATE

MISSION SPECIALIST
RARITY: EPIC
SET: SPACE EXPLORERS

MOONWALKER
RARITY: EPIC
SET: SPACE EXPLORERS

POWER CHORD
RARITY: LEGENDARY
SET: VOLUME 11

RABBIT RAIDER
RARITY: EPIC
SET: PASTEL PATROL

RADIANT STRIKER
RARITY: RARE

RAVEN
RARITY: LEGENDARY
SET: NEVERMORE

REX
RARITY: LEGENDARY
SET: DINO GUARD

ROGUE AGENT
RARITY: EPIC
SET: BLACK VECTOR

RUST LORD
RARITY: EPIC
SET: STORM SCAVENGER

SASH SERGEANT
RARITY: RARE

SCARLET DEFENDER
RARITY: UNCOMMON

SGT. GREEN CLOVER
RARITY: UNCOMMON
SET: GREEN CLOVER

SPLODE
RARITY: EPIC
SET: SHORT FUSE

STEELSIGHT
RARITY: EPIC

SUB COMMANDER
RARITY: EPIC

TOMATOHEAD
RARITY: EPIC
SET: PIZZA PIT

TOWER RECON SPECIALIST
RARITY: UNCOMMON

TRICERA OPS
RARITY: LEGENDARY
SET: DINO GUARD

WHIPLASH
RARITY: UNCOMMON
SET: RACER ROYALE

ASTRO
RARITY: EPIC
SET: SPACE EXPLORERS

BACKUP PLAN
RARITY: LEGENDARY

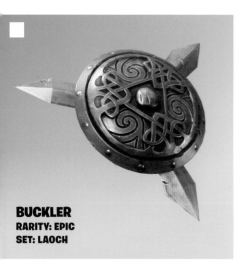

BUCKLER
RARITY: EPIC
SET: LAOCH

CATALYST
RARITY: EPIC

DARK MATTER
RARITY: LEGENDARY
SET: SPACE EXPLORERS

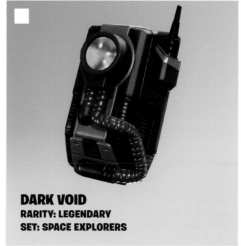

DARK VOID
RARITY: LEGENDARY
SET: SPACE EXPLORERS

EGGSHELL
RARITY: EPIC
SET: PASTEL PATROL

FISH TANK
RARITY: LEGENDARY
SET: SPACE EXPLORERS

FOXPACK
RARITY: RARE
SET: FUR FORCE

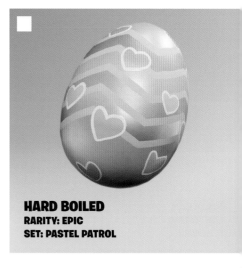

HARD BOILED
RARITY: EPIC
SET: PASTEL PATROL

HATCHLING
RARITY: LEGENDARY
SET: DINO GUARD

IRON CAGE
RARITY: LEGENDARY
SET: NEVERMORE

PRECISION
RARITY: RARE
SET: BLACK VECTOR

RUST BUCKET
RARITY: EPIC
SET: STORM SCAVENGER

SCALY
RARITY: LEGENDARY
SET: DINO GUARD

SPECIAL DELIVERY
RARITY: EPIC
SET: PIZZA PIT

STEELCAST
RARITY: EPIC

ANARCHY AXE
RARITY: RARE
SET: VOLUME 11

AXERONI
RARITY: RARE
SET: PIZZA PIT

BITEMARK
RARITY: EPIC
SET: DINO GUARD

CARROT STICK
RARITY: RARE
SET: PASTEL PATROL

CUTTING EDGE
RARITY: RARE
SET: OVERCLOCKED

EMPIRE AXE
RARITY: RARE

EVA
RARITY: EPIC
SET: SPACE EXPLORERS

GLOBAL AXE
RARITY: EPIC

INSTIGATOR
RARITY: RARE

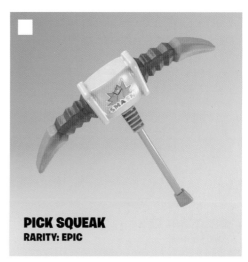

PICK SQUEAK
RARITY: EPIC

POT O' GOLD
RARITY: EPIC
SET: GREEN CLOVER

RAINBOW SMASH
RARITY: EPIC
SET: SUNSHINE & RAINBOWS

SAWTOOTH
RARITY: RARE
SET: STORM SCAVENGER

SILVER FANG
RARITY: RARE
SET: LAOCH

SPECTRAL AXE
RARITY: RARE

SPECTRE
RARITY: RARE
SET: STEALTH SYNDICATE

TACTICAL SPADE
RARITY: UNCOMMON
SET: BLACK VECTOR

CARBON
RARITY: UNCOMMON
SET: BLACK VECTOR

CHECKER
RARITY: UNCOMMON
SET: RACER ROYALE

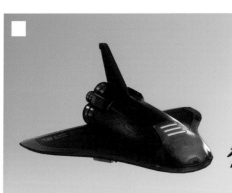

DEEP SPACE LANDER
RARITY: EPIC
SET: SPACE EXPLORERS

FEATHERED FLYER
RARITY: RARE
SET: NEVERMORE

FOSSIL FLYER
RARITY: UNCOMMON
SET: DINO GUARD

GOOGLY
RARITY: RARE

ORBITAL SHUTTLE
RARITY: EPIC
SET: SPACE EXPLORERS

PAPER PARASOL
RARITY: COMMON

PLANETARY PROBE
RARITY: EPIC
SET: SPACE EXPLORERS

RAINBOW RIDER
RARITY: RARE
SET: SUNSHINE & RAINBOWS

ROYALE DRAGON
RARITY: LEGENDARY

RUSTY RIDER
RARITY: EPIC
SET: STORM SCAVENGER

SLIPSTREAM
RARITY: EPIC

STAGE DIVE
RARITY: RARE
SET: VOLUME 11

STORM SIGIL
RARITY: UNCOMMON
SET: LAOCH

FORTNITE FACTS
ROYALE DRAGON WAS THE FIRST LEGENDARY GLIDER IN FORTNITE. RELEASED TO CELEBRATE CHINESE NEW YEAR 2018, THIS FEARSOME GLIDER STILL TURNS HEADS.

ALL-STAR
RARITY: RARE

BUBBLES
RARITY: RARE

FLAMES
RARITY: RARE

RAINBOW
RARITY: RARE

ULTRAMARINE
RARITY: RARE

FORTNITE FACTS
CONTRAILS WERE FIRST LAUNCHED
AS PART OF SEASON 3'S BATTLE
PASS—YOU HAD TO REACH TIER
84 TO UNLOCK FLAMES.

BEST MATES
RARITY: RARE

BREAKIN'
RARITY: EPIC

BREAKING POINT
RARITY: UNCOMMON

BRUSH YOUR SHOULDERS
RARITY: UNCOMMON

CLICK!
RARITY: UNCOMMON

CONFUSED
RARITY: RARE

DISCO FEVER
RARITY: EPIC
SET: FORTNITE FEVER

FACE PALM
RARITY: UNCOMMON

FLIPPIN' SEXY
RARITY: RARE

HOOTENANNY
RARITY: RARE

JUBILATION
RARITY: UNCOMMON

MAKE IT RAIN
RARITY: RARE

REANIMATED
RARITY: EPIC

ROCK OUT
RARITY: EPIC
SET: VOLUME 11

ROCK PAPER SCISSORS
RARITY: UNCOMMON

ROCKET RODEO
RARITY: EPIC

SALUTE
RARITY: UNCOMMON

SQUAT KICK
RARITY: EPIC

STEP IT UP
RARITY: RARE

TAKE THE L
RARITY: RARE

THE ROBOT
RARITY: EPIC

TIDY
RARITY: RARE

WIGGLE
RARITY: RARE

FORTNITE FACTS

TAKE THE L REAPPEARED AS A HOLIDAY-THEMED VERSION IN SEASON 7'S TAKE THE ELF, WITH THE HAND HOLDING MISTLETOE ABOVE THE HEAD. SEE WHAT WE DID THERE?

SEASON 4

ABSTRAKT
RARITY: EPIC
SET: AEROSOL ASSASSINS

AERIAL THREAT
RARITY: RARE
SET: GOALBOUND

BANDOLIER
RARITY: EPIC
SET: TROPIC TROOPERS

BATTLEHAWK
RARITY: EPIC
SET: ADVANCED FORCES

BLUE STRIKER
RARITY: EPIC

BUNNY BRAWLER
RARITY: EPIC
SET: PASTEL PATROL

CARBIDE
RARITY: LEGENDARY
SET: CARBIDE

CHROMIUM
RARITY: RARE
SET: SOLID STEEL

CLINICAL CROSSER
RARITY: RARE
SET: GOALBOUND

CRITERION
RARITY: LEGENDARY
SET: CRITERION

DIECAST
RARITY: RARE
SET: SOLID STEEL

DYNAMIC DRIBBLER
RARITY: RARE
SET: GOALBOUND

FATE
RARITY: LEGENDARY
SET: OVERSEER

FINESSE FINISHER
RARITY: RARE
SET: GOALBOUND

FIREWORKS TEAM LEADER
RARITY: EPIC
SET: STARS & STRIPES

FLYTRAP
RARITY: LEGENDARY
SET: FLYTRAP

GUMSHOE
RARITY: EPIC
SET: HARDBOILED

HAZARD AGENT
RARITY: EPIC
SET: OUTBREAK

JUMPSHOT
RARITY: RARE
SET: HALF COURT

LITESHOW
RARITY: UNCOMMON
SET: NEON GLOW

MIDFIELD MAESTRO
RARITY: RARE
SET: GOALBOUND

MOISTY MERMAN
RARITY: LEGENDARY

NITELITE
RARITY: UNCOMMON
SET: NEON GLOW

NOIR
RARITY: EPIC
SET: HARDBOILED

OBLIVION
RARITY: LEGENDARY
SET: OBLIVION

OMEGA
RARITY: LEGENDARY
SET: OMEGA

OMEN
RARITY: LEGENDARY
SET: OVERSEER

POISED PLAYMAKER
RARITY: RARE
SET: GOALBOUND

RAPSCALLION
RARITY: EPIC
SET: JAILBIRD

SCOUNDREL
RARITY: EPIC
SET: JAILBIRD

SKY STALKER
RARITY: LEGENDARY
SET: SKY STALKER

SLEUTH
RARITY: EPIC
SET: HARDBOILED

SQUAD LEADER
RARITY: EPIC
SET: ADVANCED FORCES

STALWART SWEEPER
RARITY: RARE
SET: GOALBOUND

STAR-SPANGLED RANGER
RARITY: UNCOMMON
SET: STARS & STRIPES

STAR-SPANGLED TROOPER
RARITY: UNCOMMON
SET: STARS & STRIPES

SUPER STRIKER
RARITY: RARE
SET: GOALBOUND

TEKNIQUE
RARITY: EPIC
SET: AEROSOL

THE VISITOR
RARITY: LEGENDARY

TOXIC TROOPER
RARITY: EPIC
SET: OUTBREAK

TRAILBLAZER
RARITY: EPIC
SET: ADVANCED FORCES

TRIPLE THREAT
RARITY: RARE
SET: HALF COURT

VALOR
RARITY: LEGENDARY
SET: VALIANT

VENTURA
RARITY: EPIC
SET: VENTURE

VENTURION
RARITY: EPIC
SET: VENTURE

VERTEX
RARITY: LEGENDARY
SET: APEX PROTOCOL

WINGMAN
RARITY: EPIC

ZOEY
RARITY: EPIC
SET: SWEET TOOTH

FORTNITE FACTS

THE VISITOR COULD BE OBTAINED AFTER COMPLETING ALL SEASON 4'S BLOCKBUSTER CHALLENGES. THIS MYSTERIOUS FIGURE FIRST EMERGED IN A METEOR SHOWER AND WAS LATER REVEALED TO BE ONE OF "THE SEVEN," ALONG WITH THE SCIENTIST FROM SEASON X.

BATTLE SHROUD
RARITY: LEGENDARY
SET: OVERSEER

BLASTING CAP
RARITY: EPIC
SET: STARS & STRIPES

BLUE SHIFT
RARITY: EPIC

BOGEY BAG
RARITY: EPIC

BOMBER BAG
RARITY: LEGENDARY

BURGLE BAG
RARITY: EPIC
SET: JAILBIRD

CLUEFINDER
RARITY: EPIC
SET: HARDBOILED

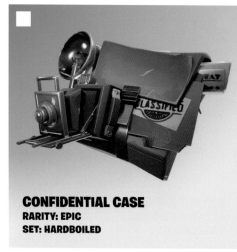

CONFIDENTIAL CASE
RARITY: EPIC
SET: HARDBOILED

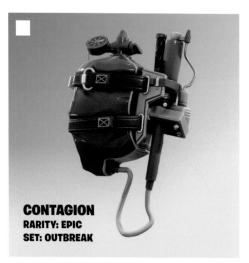

CONTAGION
RARITY: EPIC
SET: OUTBREAK

CRESTED CAPE
RARITY: LEGENDARY
SET: LAOCH

DEFLECTOR
RARITY: LEGENDARY
SET: APEX PROTOCOL

DESTABILIZER
RARITY: LEGENDARY
SET: OBLIVION

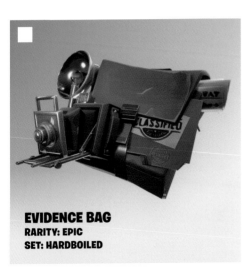

EVIDENCE BAG
RARITY: EPIC
SET: HARDBOILED

GOODIE BAG
RARITY: EPIC
SET: SWEET TOOTH

LAST GASP
RARITY: LEGENDARY
SET: SKY STALKER

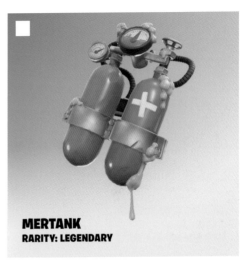

MERTANK
RARITY: LEGENDARY

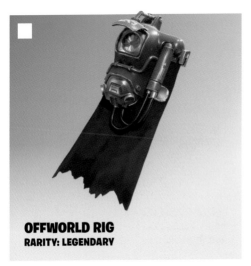

OFFWORLD RIG
RARITY: LEGENDARY

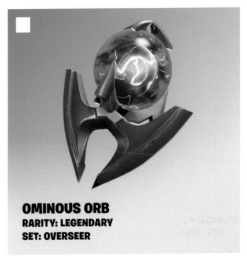

OMINOUS ORB
RARITY: LEGENDARY
SET: OVERSEER

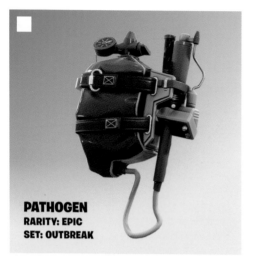

PATHOGEN
RARITY: EPIC
SET: OUTBREAK

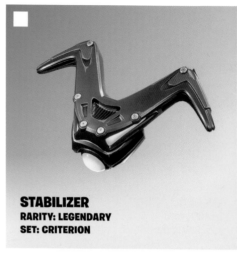

STABILIZER
RARITY: LEGENDARY
SET: CRITERION

STANDARD ISSUE
RARITY: RARE
SET: ADVANCED FORCES

STRONGBOX
RARITY: EPIC
SET: JAILBIRD

TAG BAG
RARITY: EPIC
SET: AEROSOL ASSASSINS

TRUE NORTH
RARITY: EPIC
SET: ADVANCED FORCES

VENTURA CAPE
RARITY: EPIC
SET: VENTURE

VENTURION CAPE
RARITY: EPIC
SET: VENTURE

FORTNITE FACTS
THE OFFWORLD RIG BACK BLING
COULD BE OBTAINED AS A
REWARD FOR COMPLETING ALL
SEVEN SEASON 4 BLOCKBUSTER
CHALLENGES. IT WAS BUNDLED
WITH THE VISITOR OUTFIT.

93

AIRFOIL
RARITY: RARE
SET: VENTURE

AUTOCLEAVE
RARITY: RARE
SET: OUTBREAK

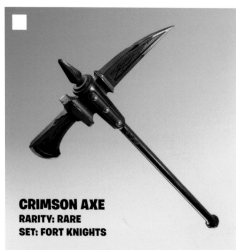

CRIMSON AXE
RARITY: RARE
SET: FORT KNIGHTS

DIRECTOR'S CUT
RARITY: RARE

ELITE CLEAT
RARITY: UNCOMMON
SET: GOALBOUND

FATED FRAME
RARITY: RARE
SET: OVERSEER

GALE FORCE
RARITY: RARE
SET: VALIANT

GLOW STICK
RARITY: RARE
SET: NEON GLOW

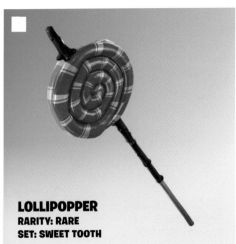

LOLLIPOPPER
RARITY: RARE
SET: SWEET TOOTH

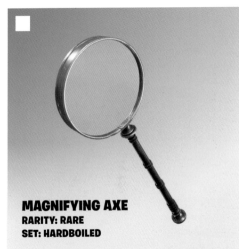

MAGNIFYING AXE
RARITY: RARE
SET: HARDBOILED

NITE OWL
RARITY: RARE
SET: JAILBIRD

ONSLAUGHT
RARITY: EPIC
SET: OMEGA

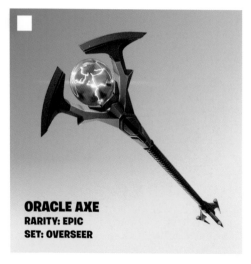

ORACLE AXE
RARITY: EPIC
SET: OVERSEER

PERSUADER
RARITY: RARE
SET: SOLID STEEL

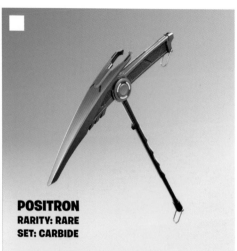

POSITRON
RARITY: RARE
SET: CARBIDE

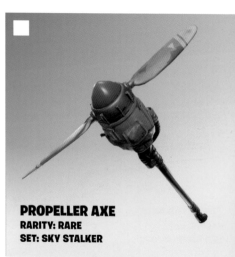

PROPELLER AXE
RARITY: RARE
SET: SKY STALKER

RAZOR EDGE
RARITY: RARE
SET: APEX PROTOCOL

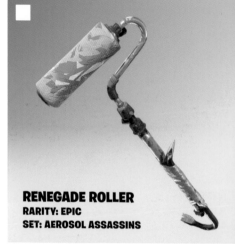

RENEGADE ROLLER
RARITY: EPIC
SET: AEROSOL ASSASSINS

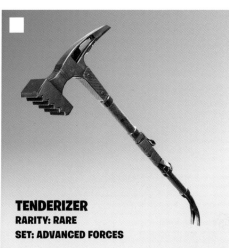

SLAM DUNK
RARITY: RARE
SET: HALF COURT

STOP AXE
RARITY: RARE

TENDERIZER
RARITY: RARE
SET: ADVANCED FORCES

TENDRIL
RARITY: RARE
SET: FLYTRAP

VICTORY LAP
RARITY: UNCOMMON
SET: RACER ROYALE

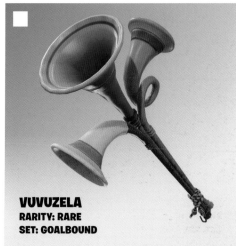

VUVUZELA
RARITY: RARE
SET: GOALBOUND

FORERUNNER
RARITY: RARE
SET: APEX PROTOCOL

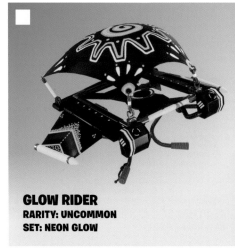

GLOW RIDER
RARITY: UNCOMMON
SET: NEON GLOW

GOALBOUND
RARITY: UNCOMMON
SET: GOALBOUND

HANG TIME
RARITY: EPIC
SET: HALF COURT

INTREPID
RARITY: EPIC
SET: CARBIDE

MAINFRAME
RARITY: UNCOMMON
SET: OVERCLOCKED

MELTDOWN
RARITY: UNCOMMON
SET: OUTBREAK

PTERODACTYL
RARITY: EPIC
SET: DINO GUARD

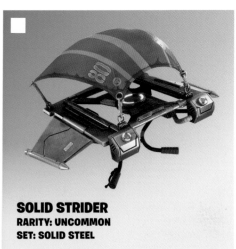

SOLID STRIDER
RARITY: UNCOMMON
SET: SOLID STEEL

SPLIT WING
RARITY: EPIC
SET: OVERSEER

STARRY FLIGHT
RARITY: RARE
SET: JAILBIRD

SUGAR CRASH
RARITY: RARE
SET: SWEET TOOTH

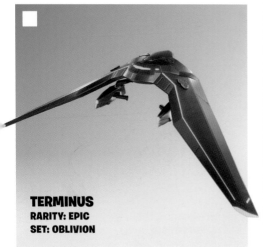

TERMINUS
RARITY: EPIC
SET: OBLIVION

TRIUMPH
RARITY: UNCOMMON
SET: VENTURE

VENUS FLYER
RARITY: EPIC
SET: FLYTRAP

VICEROY MARK I
RARITY: EPIC
SET: HARDBOILED

WET PAINT
RARITY: COMMON

WINGS OF VALOR
RARITY: EPIC
SET: VALIANT

HEARTS
RARITY: RARE

LIGHTNING
RARITY: RARE

RETRO SCI-FI
RARITY: RARE

SHOOTING STAR
RARITY: RARE

SPRAY PAINT
RARITY: RARE

FORTNITE FACTS
SHOOTING STAR CREATES A BLUE FLAME EFFECT AS YOU SKYDIVE, MIMICKING AN OBJECT ENTERING THE ATMOSPHERE.

BALLER
RARITY: RARE

BONELESS
RARITY: RARE

BRING IT
RARITY: UNCOMMON

CHICKEN
RARITY: RARE

DIP
RARITY: UNCOMMON

EAGLE
RARITY: RARE

GROOVE JAM
RARITY: EPIC

HYPE
RARITY: RARE

INFINITE DAB
RARITY: RARE

KICK UPS
RARITY: RARE

LAUGH IT UP
RARITY: RARE

ORANGE JUSTICE
RARITY: RARE

POP LOCK
RARITY: EPIC

POPCORN
RARITY: RARE

RAMBUNCTIOUS
RARITY: RARE

RAWR
RARITY: RARE

RED CARD
RARITY: UNCOMMON

RESPECT
RARITY: UNCOMMON

ROCKET SPINNER
RARITY: RARE

SNAP
RARITY: UNCOMMON

SPARKLER
RARITY: UNCOMMON

STAR POWER
RARITY: EPIC

TAKE 14
RARITY: UNCOMMON

THUMBS DOWN
RARITY: UNCOMMON

THUMBS UP
RARITY: UNCOMMON

TRUE HEART
RARITY: EPIC

WATERWORKS
RARITY: UNCOMMON

ZANY
RARITY: RARE

FORTNITE FACTS
**YOU'D NEED TO REACH TIER 95 OF
SEASON 4'S BATTLE PASS TO WIN
THE SERIOUSLY FUNKY GROOVE
JAM EMOTE.**

SEASON 5

AEROBIC ASSASSIN
RARITY: EPIC
SET: SPANDEX SQUAD

ARCHETYPE
RARITY: EPIC
SET: ARCHETYPE

DILLO
UNCOMMON

BACKBONE
RARITY: RARE
SET: BIKER BRIGADE

BEEF BOSS
RARITY: EPIC
SET: DURRR BURGER

CHOMP SR.
RARITY: LEGENDARY
SET: CHOMP

CHOPPER
RARITY: RARE
SET: BIKER BRIGADE

CLOAKED STAR
RARITY: EPIC

DREAMFLOWER
RARITY: EPIC
SET: FLOWER POWER

DRIFT
RARITY: LEGENDARY
SET: DRIFT

DYNAMO
RARITY: RARE
SET: LUCHA

ENFORCER
RARITY: LEGENDARY

FAR OUT MAN
RARITY: EPIC
SET: FLOWER POWER

FIELD SURGEON
RARITY: EPIC
SET: SUPPORT SQUADRON

FORTUNE
RARITY: RARE
SET: SHARP STYLE

GALAXY
RARITY: EPIC
SET: GALAXY

GARRISON
RARITY: UNCOMMON

GRILL SERGEANT
RARITY: UNCOMMON
SET: DURRR BURGER

HACIVAT
RARITY: EPIC
SET: HACIVAT

HIME
RARITY: LEGENDARY
SET: BUSHIDO

HUNTRESS
RARITY: EPIC
SET: NORSE

MAGNUS
RARITY: LEGENDARY
SET: NORSE

MASKED FURY
RARITY: RARE
SET: LUCHA

MAVERICK
RARITY: EPIC
SET: COBRA CREW

MONIKER
RARITY: RARE
SET: SHARP STYLE

MULLET MARAUDER
RARITY: EPIC
SET: SPANDEX SQUAD

MUSHA
RARITY: LEGENDARY
SET: BUSHIDO

NITE NITE
RARITY: EPIC
SET: PARTY PARADE

OVERTAKER
RARITY: EPIC
SET: VANISHING POINT

P.A.N.D.A. TEAM LEADER
RARITY: LEGENDARY

PEEKABOO
RARITY: EPIC
SET: PARTY PARADE

RAGNAROK
RARITY: LEGENDARY
SET: HARBINGER

RAVAGE
RARITY: LEGENDARY
SET: NEVERMORE

REDLINE
RARITY: EPIC
SET: RPM

REEF RANGER
RARITY: EPIC
SET: DIVEMASTERS

ROOK
RARITY: EPIC

ROSE TEAM LEADER
RARITY: LEGENDARY
SET: ROSE TEAM

ROYALE BOMBER
RARITY: EPIC

SCORPION
RARITY: UNCOMMON

SHADE
RARITY: EPIC
SET: COBRA CREW

SLEDGEHAMMER
RARITY: EPIC
SET: ADVANCED FORCES

STAGE SLAYER
RARITY: EPIC
SET: GARAGE BAND

SUN STRIDER
RARITY: EPIC
SET: RESCUE PATROL

SUN TAN SPECIALIST
RARITY: EPIC
SET: RESCUE PATROL

SUSHI MASTER
RARITY: RARE
SET: SUSHI

SYNTH STAR
RARITY: EPIC
SET: GARAGE BAND

THE ACE
RARITY: EPIC
SET: GETAWAY GANG

TRIAGE TROOPER
RARITY: EPIC
SET: SUPPORT SQUADRON

119

VALKYRIE
RARITY: LEGENDARY
SET: HARBINGER

WARPAINT
RARITY: LEGENDARY
SET: WARPAINT

WAYPOINT
RARITY: RARE
SET: WAYPOINT

WHITEOUT
RARITY: EPIC
SET: VANISHING POINT

WILD CARD
RARITY: LEGENDARY
SET: GETAWAY GANG

WRECK RAIDER
RARITY: EPIC
SET: DIVEMASTERS

FORTNITE FACTS
**MUSHA AND HIME MEAN
"WARRIOR" AND "PRINCESS"
IN JAPANESE. THESE OUTFITS
ARE BASED ON TRADITIONAL
SAMURAI COSTUMES FROM
FEUDAL JAPAN.**

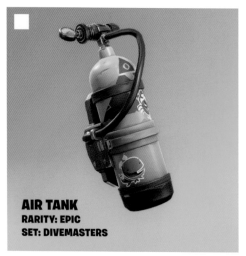

AIR TANK
RARITY: EPIC
SET: DIVEMASTERS

BALLISTIC
RARITY: EPIC
SET: COBRA CREW

BALLOON LLAMA
RARITY: EPIC
SET: PARTY PARADE

BAMBOO
RARITY: LEGENDARY

BAT ATTITUDE
RARITY: EPIC
SET: COBRA CREW

BATTLE BALLOON
RARITY: EPIC
SET: PARTY PARADE

BIRTHDAY CAKE
RARITY: RARE

BOOMBOX
RARITY: EPIC
SET: SPANDEX SQUAD

BUCKLED
RARITY: UNCOMMON

CARE PACKAGE
RARITY: EPIC
SET: SUPPORT SQUADRON

CHEF'S CHOICE
RARITY: RARE
SET: SUSHI

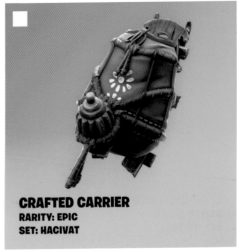

CRAFTED CARRIER
RARITY: EPIC
SET: HACIVAT

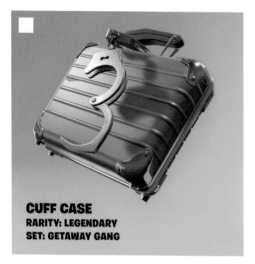

CUFF CASE
RARITY: LEGENDARY
SET: GETAWAY GANG

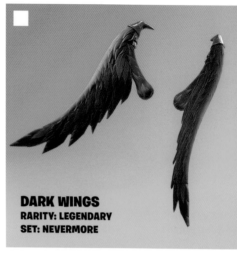

DARK WINGS
RARITY: LEGENDARY
SET: NEVERMORE

DEEP FRIED
RARITY: EPIC
SET: DURRR BURGER

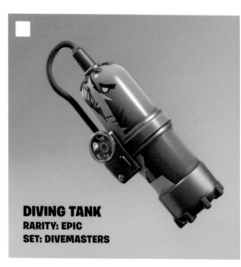

DIVING TANK
RARITY: EPIC
SET: DIVEMASTERS

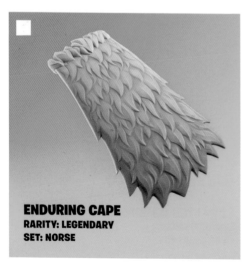

ENDURING CAPE
RARITY: LEGENDARY
SET: NORSE

FROZEN SHROUD
RARITY: LEGENDARY
SET: HARBINGER

GURNEY GEAR
RARITY: EPIC
SET: SUPPORT SQUADRON

HIP SHAKERS
RARITY: EPIC
SET: FLOWER POWER

IGNITION
RARITY: EPIC
SET: VANISHING POINT

INSIGNIA
RARITY: RARE

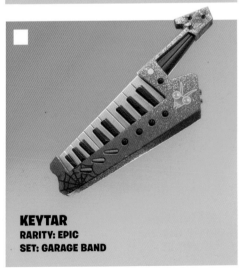

KEYTAR
RARITY: EPIC
SET: GARAGE BAND

KICK DRUM
RARITY: EPIC
SET: GARAGE BAND

LANE SPLITTER
RARITY: EPIC
SET: VANISHING POINT

PARADIGM
RARITY: EPIC
SET: ARCHETYPE

PENGUIN
RARITY: RARE

POOL PARTY
RARITY: EPIC
SET: RESCUE PATROL

PURSUIT
RARITY: LEGENDARY
SET: WARPAINT

REARGUARD
RARITY: EPIC
SET: NORSE

RESCUE RING
RARITY: EPIC
SET: RESCUE PATROL

ROAD FLAIR
RARITY: RARE
SET: BIKER BRIGADE

ROAD READY
RARITY: RARE
SET: BIKER BRIGADE

SASHIMONO
RARITY: LEGENDARY
SET: BUSHIDO

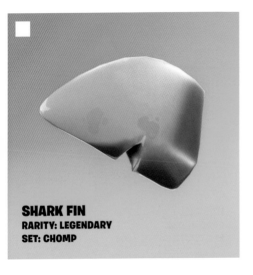

SHARK FIN
RARITY: LEGENDARY
SET: CHOMP

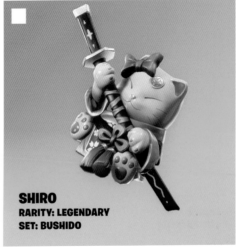

SHIRO
RARITY: LEGENDARY
SET: BUSHIDO

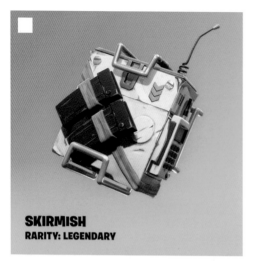

SKIRMISH
RARITY: LEGENDARY

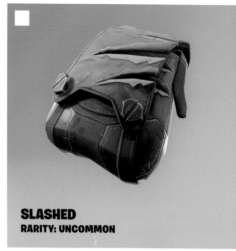

SLASHED
RARITY: UNCOMMON

SUBJUGATOR
RARITY: LEGENDARY

SUMMER STRUMMER
RARITY: EPIC
SET: FLOWER POWER

SWAG BAG
RARITY: EPIC
SET: GETAWAY GANG

UPLINK
RARITY: EPIC
SET: ADVANCED FORCES

VALKYRIE WINGS
RARITY: LEGENDARY
SET: HARBINGER

VINTAGE
RARITY: UNCOMMON

FORTNITE FACTS

THE BIRTHDAY CAKE BACK
BLING WAS RELEASED AS PART
OF FORTNITE'S FIRST BIRTHDAY
CELEBRATION IN JULY 2018, AS ONE
OF THE PRIZES FOR COMPLETING ALL
THREE BIRTHDAY CHALLENGES.

AXERCISE
RARITY: UNCOMMON
SET: SPANDEX SQUAD

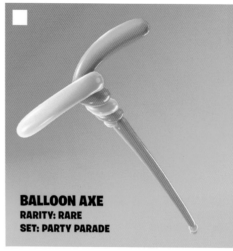

BALLOON AXE
RARITY: RARE
SET: PARTY PARADE

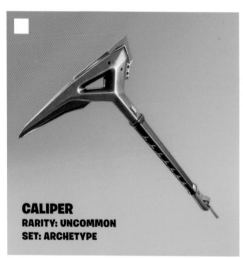

CALIPER
RARITY: UNCOMMON
SET: ARCHETYPE

CAT'S CLAW
RARITY: RARE
SET: BUSHIDO

CLUTCH AXE
RARITY: RARE
SET: COBRA CREW

CONTROLLER
RARITY: EPIC

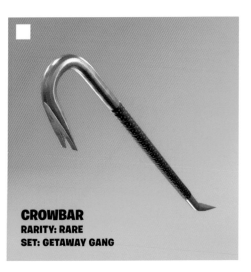

CROWBAR
RARITY: RARE
SET: GETAWAY GANG

DRUMBEAT
RARITY: UNCOMMON
SET: FLOWER POWER

FILET AXE
RARITY: RARE
SET: SUSHI

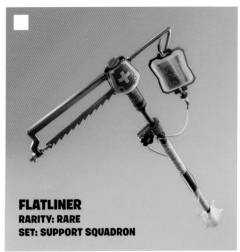

FLATLINER
RARITY: RARE
SET: SUPPORT SQUADRON

FOREBEARER
RARITY: RARE
SET: NORSE

HARPOON AXE
RARITY: RARE
SET: DIVEMASTERS

IRON BEAK
RARITY: RARE
SET: NEVERMORE

JINGU BANG
RARITY: EPIC
SET: WUKONG

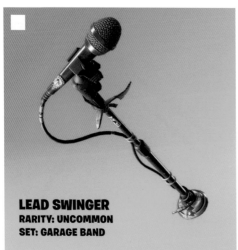

LEAD SWINGER
RARITY: UNCOMMON
SET: GARAGE BAND

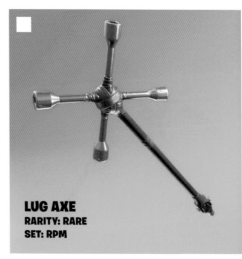

LUG AXE
RARITY: RARE
SET: RPM

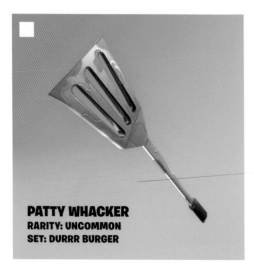

PATTY WHACKER
RARITY: UNCOMMON
SET: DURRR BURGER

PERMAFROST
RARITY: EPIC
SET: HARBINGER

PILEDRIVER
RARITY: RARE
SET: LUCHA

POINTER
RARITY: RARE

POWER GRIP
RARITY: RARE

RESCUE PADDLE
RARITY: RARE
SET: RESCUE PATROL

RIFT EDGE
RARITY: EPIC
SET: DRIFT

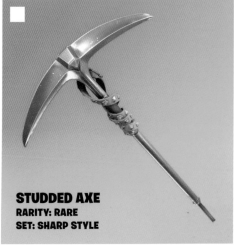

STUDDED AXE
RARITY: RARE
SET: SHARP STYLE

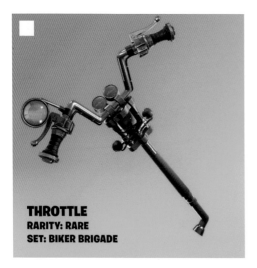

THROTTLE
RARITY: RARE
SET: BIKER BRIGADE

TREE SPLITTER
RARITY: UNCOMMON
SET: HACIVAT

FORTNITE FACTS
COMPLETING ALL THREE CHALLENGES IN SEASON 5'S HIGH STAKES EVENT WOULD UNLOCK THE CROWBAR HARVESTING TOOL, PART OF THE GETAWAY GANG SET.

AIRLIFT
RARITY: EPIC
SET: SUPPORT SQUADRON

BEACH UMBRELLA
RARITY: COMMON

BLAZE
RARITY: UNCOMMON
SET: BIKER BRIGADE

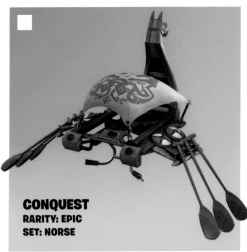

CONQUEST
RARITY: EPIC
SET: NORSE

CRUISER
RARITY: UNCOMMON
SET: COBRA CREW

CYCLONE
RARITY: EPIC
SET: RPM

DOWNSHIFT
RARITY: UNCOMMON
SET: RPM

FLAPPY
RARITY: RARE

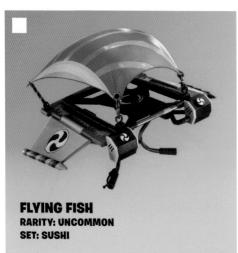

FLYING FISH
RARITY: UNCOMMON
SET: SUSHI

FLYING SAUCER
RARITY: EPIC
SET: DURRR BURGER

FROSTWING
RARITY: LEGENDARY
SET: HARBINGER

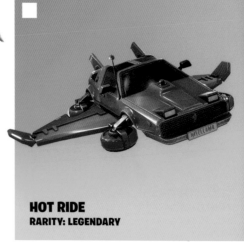

HOT RIDE
RARITY: LEGENDARY

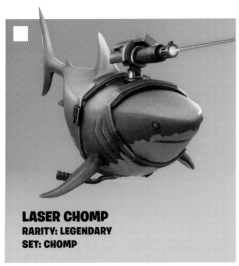

LASER CHOMP
RARITY: LEGENDARY
SET: CHOMP

LIBRE
RARITY: RARE
SET: LUCHA

PURRFECT
RARITY: UNCOMMON
SET: BUSHIDO

RHINESTONE RIDER
RARITY: UNCOMMON
SET: SHARP STYLE

SAFECRACKER
RARITY: RARE
SET: GETAWAY GANG

SERVO
RARITY: EPIC
SET: ARCHETYPE

SHADOW PUPPET
RARITY: EPIC
SET: HACIVAT

SPLASHDOWN
RARITY: EPIC
SET: RESCUE PATROL

TIE-DYE FLYER
RARITY: RARE
SET: FLOWER POWER

WHITE SQUALL
RARITY: EPIC
SET: VANISHING POINT

WINDBREAKER
RARITY: UNCOMMON
SET: SPANDEX SQUAD

ARTIFACT
RARITY: RARE

CASH FLOW
RARITY: RARE
SET: GETAWAY GANG

DARK FEATHERS
RARITY: RARE
SET: NEVERMORE

EMBERS
RARITY: RARE

GLITCH IN THE SYSTEM
RARITY: RARE

ICE CRYSTALS
RARITY: RARE

LANTERNS
RARITY: RARE

RUNIC
RARITY: RARE

TP
RARITY: RARE

SEASON 5 **EMOTES**

BATTLE CALL
RARITY: UNCOMMON

BOOGIE DOWN
RARITY: EPIC

BREAKDOWN
RARITY: EPIC

2+2=4

CALCULATED
RARITY: RARE

CAPOEIRA
RARITY: RARE

DANCE THERAPY
RARITY: EPIC

FANCY FEET
RARITY: RARE

FINGER WAG
RARITY: UNCOMMON

FIST PUMP
RARITY: UNCOMMON

FLIPPIN' INCREDIBLE
RARITY: RARE

FREESTYLIN'
RARITY: EPIC

GENTLEMAN'S DAB
RARITY: UNCOMMON

GO! GO! GO!
RARITY: UNCOMMON

HAND SIGNALS
RARITY: RARE

HITCHHIKER
RARITY: RARE

HOT STUFF
RARITY: UNCOMMON

HULA
RARITY: EPIC

INTENSITY
RARITY: EPIC

JOB WELL DONE
RARITY: UNCOMMON

LIVING LARGE
RARITY: RARE

LLAMA BELL
RARITY: EPIC

MY IDOL!
RARITY: UNCOMMON

ON THE HOOK
RARITY: RARE

PRAISE THE TOMATO
RARITY: RARE

PUMPERNICKEL
RARITY: RARE

SHAKE IT UP
RARITY: EPIC

SWIPE IT
RARITY: RARE

TWIST
RARITY: RARE

VIVACIOUS
RARITY: EPIC

WORK IT OUT
RARITY: RARE

YOU'RE AWESOME
RARITY: RARE

FORTNITE FACTS

**FREESTYLIN' WAS ONLY AVAILABLE VIA THE
SECOND TWITCH PRIME PACK, ALONG WITH
THE TRAILBLAZER OUTFIT, TRUE NORTH BACK
BLING, AND TENDERIZER HARVESTING TOOL.**

63 skins
45 back blings
~~XXXXXXXX~~
36 harvesting tools
21 gliders
6 contrails
28 emotes

SEASON 6

A.I.M.
RARITY: LEGENDARY
SET: A.I.M.

AIRHEART
RARITY: RARE
SET: AVIATION AGE

ARACHNE
RARITY: LEGENDARY
SET: ARACHNID

BLITZ
RARITY: EPIC
SET: FOURTH DOWN

BRAINIAC
RARITY: UNCOMMON

BULLSEYE
RARITY: UNCOMMON
SET: BULLSEYE

BUNNYMOON
RARITY: UNCOMMON

CALAMITY
RARITY: LEGENDARY
SET: WESTERN WILDS

CASTOR
RARITY: EPIC
SET: ARCANE ARTS

DANTE
RARITY: EPIC
SET: MUERTOS

ARK BOMBER
DARK
NG & THUNDERSTORMS

DEADFIRE
RARITY: LEGENDARY
SET: WESTERN WILDS

DIRE
RARITY: LEGENDARY
SET: FULL MOON

DJ YONDER
RARITY: EPIC
SET: TWIN TURNTABLES

DOUBLE HELIX
RARITY: EPIC
SET: DOUBLE HELIX

DUSK
RARITY: EPIC
SET: NITE COVEN

ELMIRA
RARITY: EPIC
SET: ARCANE ARTS

END ZONE
RARITY: EPIC
SET: FOURTH DOWN

EON
RARITY: LEGENDARY
SET: EON

FABLE
RARITY: EPIC
SET: RED RIDING

FLAPJACKIE
RARITY: EPIC
SET: ANIMAL JACKETS

FROSTBITE
RARITY: LEGENDARY
SET: DEEP FREEZE

GIDDY-UP
RARITY: EPIC

GRIDIRON
RARITY: EPIC
SET: FOURTH DOWN

GROWLER
RARITY: EPIC
SET: ANIMAL JACKETS

GUAN YU
RARITY: EPIC
SET: GUAN YU

HAY MAN
RARITY: EPIC
SET: STUFFED

HEIDI
RARITY: EPIC
SET: OKTOBERFEST

HOLLOWHEAD
RARITY: EPIC
SET: PUMPKIN PATCH

INTERCEPTOR
RARITY: EPIC
SET: FOURTH DOWN

JACK GOURDON
RARITY: EPIC
SET: PUMPKIN PATCH

JUKE
RARITY: EPIC
SET: FOURTH DOWN

LUDWIG
RARITY: EPIC
SET: OKTOBERFEST

MAKI MASTER
RARITY: RARE
SET: SUSHI

MAXIMILLIAN
RARITY: RARE
SET: AVIATION AGE

MAYHEM
RARITY: RARE
SET: WASTELAND WARRIORS

MOTHMANDO
RARITY: EPIC
SET: MOTH COMMAND

NARA
RARITY: EPIC
SET: STORM FAMILIARS

NIGHTSHADE
RARITY: EPIC
SET: PIZZA PIT

PATCH PATROLLER
RARITY: UNCOMMON
SET: PUMPKIN PATCH

PLAGUE
RARITY: EPIC
SET: GRIM MEDICINE

REFLEX
RARITY: RARE
SET: COUNTERATTACK

RIOT
RARITY: RARE
SET: VOLUME 11

ROSA
RARITY: EPIC
SET: MUERTOS

RUCKUS
RARITY: RARE
SET: WASTELAND WARRIORS

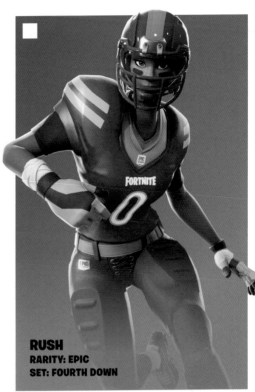

RUSH
RARITY: EPIC
SET: FOURTH DOWN

SANCTUM
RARITY: EPIC
SET: NITE COVEN

SCOURGE
RARITY: EPIC
SET: GRIM MEDICINE

SHOGUN
RARITY: LEGENDARY
SET: SHOGUN

SKULL RANGER
RARITY: RARE
SET: SKULL SQUAD

SKULL TROOPER (GREEN GLOW)
RARITY: RARE
SET: SKULL SQUAD

SKULL TROOPER (PURPLE GLOW)
RARITY: RARE
SET: SKULL SQUAD

SPIDER KNIGHT
RARITY: LEGENDARY
SET: ARACHNID

SPIKE
RARITY: EPIC
SET: FOURTH DOWN

SPOOKY TEAM LEADER
RARITY: EPIC

STRAW OPS
RARITY: EPIC
SET: STRAW STUFFED

STRIPED SOLDIER
RARITY: UNCOMMON

STRONG GUARD
RARITY: EPIC
SET: FOURTH DOWN

TRIKER

TARO
RARITY: EPIC
SET: STORM FAMILIARS

TENDER DEFENDER
RARITY: EPIC
SET: FOWL PLAY

WHISTLE WARRIOR
RARITY: UNCOMMON

YEE-HAW!
RARITY: EPIC

FORTNITE FACTS

DIRE WAS AWARDED AT TIER 100 OF THE BATTLE PASS; IT FEATURED UNLOCKABLE PROGRESSIVE STYLES THAT TRANSFORM THE OUTFIT INTO A MONSTROUS WEREWOLF.

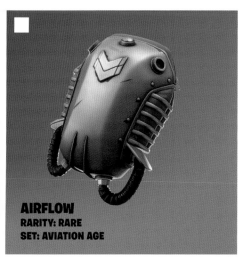

AIRFLOW
RARITY: RARE
SET: AVIATION AGE

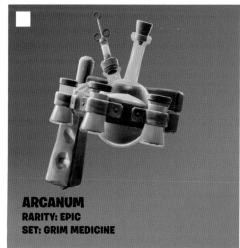

ARCANUM
RARITY: EPIC
SET: GRIM MEDICINE

BIRDHOVEL
RARITY: EPIC
SET: STRAW STUFFED

BLADED WINGS
RARITY: LEGENDARY
SET: SHOGUN

BONESY
RARITY: EPIC

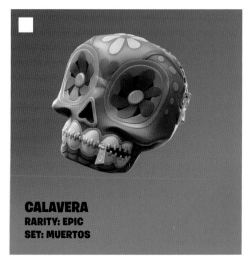

CALAVERA
RARITY: EPIC
SET: MUERTOS

CAMO
RARITY: EPIC

CLOCKWORKS
RARITY: EPIC
SET: OKTOBERFEST

COVEN CAPE
RARITY: EPIC
SET: NITE COVEN

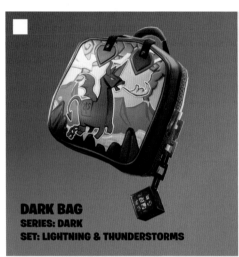

DARK BAG
SERIES: DARK
SET: LIGHTNING & THUNDERSTORMS

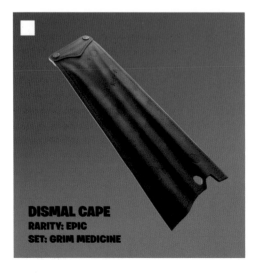

DISMAL CAPE
RARITY: EPIC
SET: GRIM MEDICINE

DUSK WINGS
RARITY: EPIC
SET: NITE COVEN

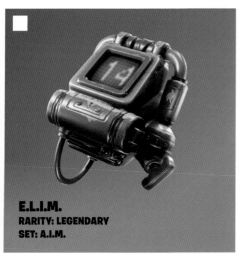

E.L.I.M.
RARITY: LEGENDARY
SET: A.I.M.

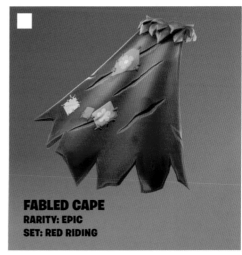

FABLED CAPE
RARITY: EPIC
SET: RED RIDING

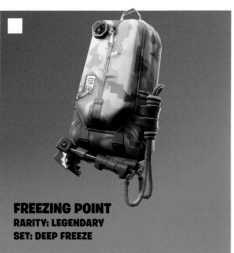

FREEZING POINT
RARITY: LEGENDARY
SET: DEEP FREEZE

GALACTIC DISC
RARITY: EPIC
SET: GALAXY

GHOST PORTAL
RARITY: EPIC
SET: GHOST SQUAD

GOODIE GOURD
RARITY: EPIC

HATCHBACK
RARITY: EPIC
SET: FOWL PLAY

HAY NEST
RARITY: EPIC
SET: STRAW STUFFED

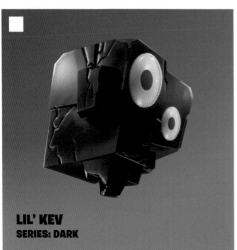

LIL' KEV
SERIES: DARK

LONG LEGS
RARITY: LEGENDARY
SET: ARACHNID

LOYAL SHIELD
RARITY: EPIC
SET: GUAN YU

MOULDERING CLOAK
RARITY: EPIC
SET: PUMPKIN PATCH

NIBBLES
RARITY: EPIC
SET: ANIMAL JACKETS

NIGHT CLOAK
RARITY: EPIC
SET: PIZZA PIT

PARA-PROVISIONS
RARITY: RARE
SET: AVIATION AGE

PRETZEL PROTECTOR
RARITY: EPIC
SET: OKTOBERFEST

PUNCTURE PACK
RARITY: RARE
SET: WASTELAND WARRIORS

SCALES
RARITY: EPIC

167

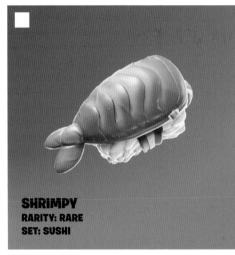

SHACKLED STONE
RARITY: LEGENDARY
SET: WESTERN WILDS

SHRIMPY
RARITY: RARE
SET: SUSHI

SPELLBINDER
RARITY: EPIC
SET: ARCANE ARTS

SPIDER SHIELD
RARITY: LEGENDARY
SET: ARACHNID

SPIKE CHAMBER
RARITY: RARE
SET: WASTELAND WARRIORS

SPIRIT CAPE
RARITY: EPIC
SET: MUERTOS

TELEMETRY
RARITY: EPIC
SET: DOUBLE HELIX

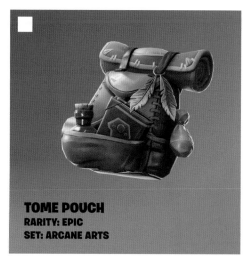

TOME POUCH
RARITY: EPIC
SET: ARCANE ARTS

TOP NOTCH
RARITY: EPIC

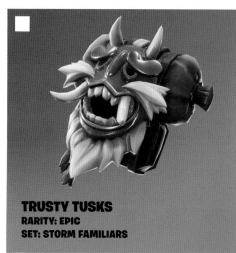

TRUSTY TUSKS
RARITY: EPIC
SET: STORM FAMILIARS

WAVEFORM
RARITY: EPIC
SET: TWIN TURNTABLES

WHITE FANG
RARITY: EPIC
SET: STORM FAMILIARS

WINGBACK
RARITY: EPIC
SET: MOTH COMMAND

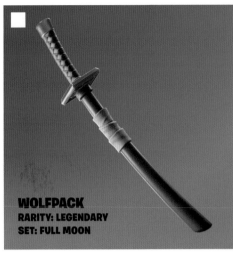

WOLFPACK
RARITY: LEGENDARY
SET: FULL MOON

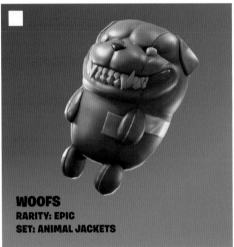

WOOFS
RARITY: EPIC
SET: ANIMAL JACKETS

FORTNITE FACTS
BONESY, CAMO, AND SCALES WERE THE FIRST PETS TO BE INTRODUCED TO FORTNITE IN SEASON 6. PETS CAN BE EQUIPPED INTO YOUR BACK BLING SLOT AND WILL REACT AS YOU PLAY.

A.X.E.
RARITY: RARE
SET: A.I.M.

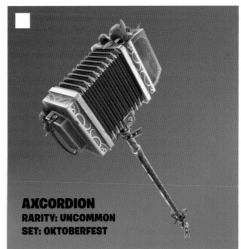

AXCORDION
RARITY: UNCOMMON
SET: OKTOBERFEST

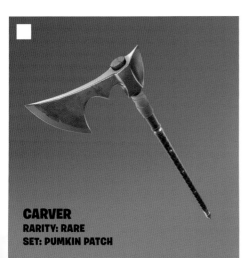

CARVER
RARITY: RARE
SET: PUMKIN PATCH

DARK SHARD
RARITY: EPIC
SET: WESTERN WILDS

FIRST DOWNER
RARITY: UNCOMMON
SET: FOURTH DOWN

GATEKEEPER
RARITY: UNCOMMON
SET: STORM FAMILIARS

171

GOLDEN PIGSKIN
RARITY: UNCOMMON
SET: FOURTH DOWN

GUANDAO
RARITY: RARE
SET: GUAN YU

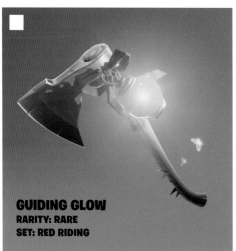

GUIDING GLOW
RARITY: RARE
SET: RED RIDING

HARVESTER
RARITY: RARE
SET: STRAW STUFFED

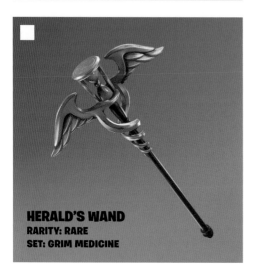

HERALD'S WAND
RARITY: RARE
SET: GRIM MEDICINE

JACKSPAMMER
RARITY: UNCOMMON
SET: ANIMAL JACKETS

JAWBLADE
RARITY: RARE
SET: SHOGUN

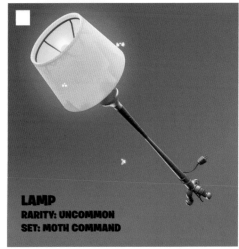

LAMP
RARITY: UNCOMMON
SET: MOTH COMMAND

MOONRISE
RARITY: EPIC
SET: NITE COVEN

NIGHT SLICER
RARITY: RARE
SET: PIZZA PIT

PINPOINT
RARITY: RARE
SET: DOUBLE HELIX

RECKONING
RARITY: EPIC
SET: WESTERN WILDS

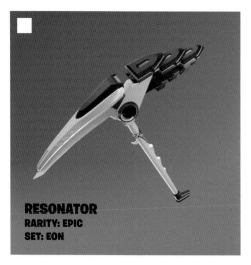

RESONATOR
RARITY: EPIC
SET: EON

SCRAMBLER
RARITY: UNCOMMON
SET: FOWL PLAY

SIX STRING STRIKER
RARITY: EPIC
SET: MUERTOS

SKULL SICKLE
RARITY: EPIC
SET: SKULL SQUAD

SMASH UP
RARITY: RARE
SET: TWIN TURNTABLES

SPELLSLINGER
RARITY: RARE
SET: ARCANE ARTS

SPLINTERSTRIKE
RARITY: RARE
SET: WASTELAND WARRIORS

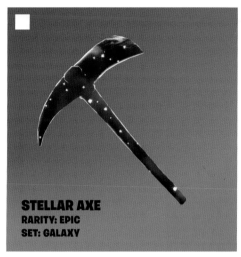

STELLAR AXE
RARITY: EPIC
SET: GALAXY

THUNDER CRASH
SERIES: DARK
SET: LIGHTNING & THUNDERSTORMS

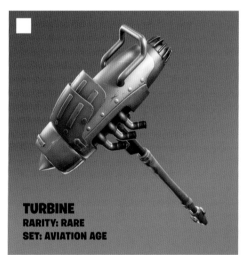

TURBINE
RARITY: RARE
SET: AVIATION AGE

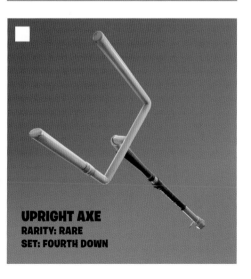

UPRIGHT AXE
RARITY: RARE
SET: FOURTH DOWN

WEB BREAKER
RARITY: RARE
SET: ARACHNID

AURORA
RARITY: EPIC
SET: EON COSMETIC

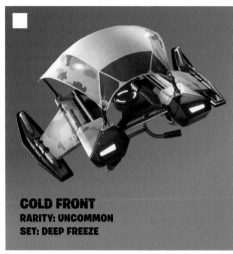

COLD FRONT
RARITY: UNCOMMON
SET: DEEP FREEZE

COVERED CRUSADER
RARITY: RARE
SET: WESTERN WILDS

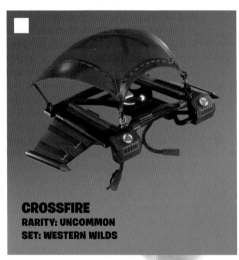

CROSSFIRE
RARITY: UNCOMMON
SET: WESTERN WILDS

CRYPT CRUISER
RARITY: EPIC
SET: SKULL SQUAD

DARK ENGINE
RARITY: EPIC
SET: WESTERN WILDS

DARK GLYPH
SERIES: DARK
SET: LIGHTNING & THUNDERSTORMS

DIRIGIBLE
RARITY: EPIC
SET: AVIATION AGE

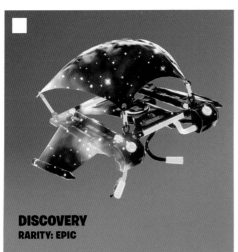

DISCOVERY
RARITY: EPIC

DIVINE DRAGON
RARITY: EPIC
SET: GUAN YU

FIELD WRAITH
RARITY: EPIC
SET: STRAW STUFFED

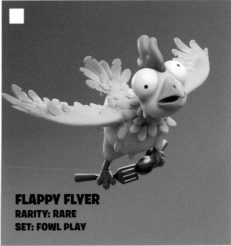

FLAPPY FLYER
RARITY: RARE
SET: FOWL PLAY

FLUTTERBUG
RARITY: RARE
SET: MOTH COMMAND

FLYING CARP
RARITY: RARE
SET: STORM FAMILIARS

HATCHLING
RARITY: EPIC
SET: ARACHNID

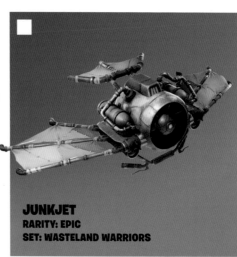

JUNKJET
RARITY: EPIC
SET: WASTELAND WARRIORS

KABUTO
RARITY: RARE
SET: SHOGUN

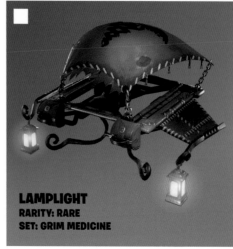

LAMPLIGHT
RARITY: RARE
SET: GRIM MEDICINE

MAGIC WINGS
RARITY: EPIC
SET: ARCANE ARTS

OKTOBERFEAST
RARITY: RARE
SET: OKTOBERFEST

PICNIC
RARITY: UNCOMMON
SET: RED RIDING

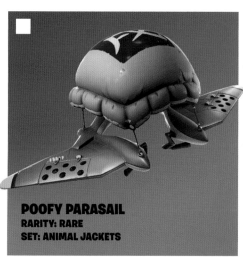

POOFY PARASAIL
RARITY: RARE
SET: ANIMAL JACKETS

ROTOR
RARITY: EPIC
SET: DOUBLE HELIX

SPIRIT
RARITY: EPIC
SET: MUERTOS

SWARM
RARITY: EPIC
SET: NITE COVEN

TOUCHDOWN
RARITY: UNCOMMON
SET: FOURTH DOWN

WEBRELLA
RARITY: COMMON

FORTNITE FACTS
DARK GLYPH IS THE ONLY GLIDER
IN FORTNITE CHAPTER 1 TO
FEATURE IN THE "DARK" SERIES.
ITEMS WITHIN SERIES DO NOT
HAVE RARITY VALUES.

BATS!
RARITY: RARE
SET: NITE COVEN

EXHAUST
RARITY: RARE
SET: AVIATION AGE

FIREFLIES
RARITY: RARE
SET: RED RIDING

JACK-O-LANTERN
RARITY: RARE

SPECTRAL ESSENCE
RARITY: RARE
SET: WESTERN WILDS

VIRULENT FLAMES
RARITY: RARE
SET: WESTERN WILDS

FORTNITE FACTS

**VIRULENT FLAMES COULD BE WON BY
COMPLETING THE FORTNITEMARES
CHALLENGES PART 3.**

BEHOLD!
RARITY: UNCOMMON

BOMBASTIC
RARITY: RARE

BUSY
RARITY: RARE

CRAZY FEET
RARITY: RARE

CRISS CROSS
RARITY: RARE

DENIED
RARITY: UNCOMMON

DROP THE BASS
RARITY: EPIC
SET: TWIN TURNTABLES

ELECTRO SWING
RARITY: RARE

FLAMENCO
RARITY: EPIC

GLITTER UP
RARITY: RARE

HEADBANGER
RARITY: RARE

HOT MARAT
RARITY: RARE

HOWL
RARITY: UNCOMMON

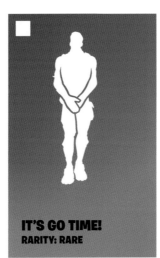

IT'S GO TIME!
RARITY: RARE

JUGGLIN'
RARITY: RARE

LLAMACADABRA
RARITY: EPIC

PHONE IT IN
RARITY: EPIC

REGAL WAVE
RARITY: UNCOMMON

RUNNING MAN
RARITY: RARE

SCORECARD
RARITY: UNCOMMON

SLITHERIN'
RARITY: RARE

SMOOTH MOVES
RARITY: EPIC

SOMETHING STINKS
RARITY: RARE

SPIKE IT
RARITY: RARE

SPRINKLER
RARITY: RARE

T-POSE
RARITY: UNCOMMON

TAI CHI
RARITY: RARE

TREAT YOURSELF
RARITY: RARE

FORTNITE FACTS
GLITTER UP WAS BUNDLED WITH THE GIDDY-UP OUTFIT AND COULD BE UNLOCKED AT TIER 23 OF THE BATTLE PASS. THE EMOTE CAN ALSO BE USED WITH THE YEE-HAW! OUTFIT.

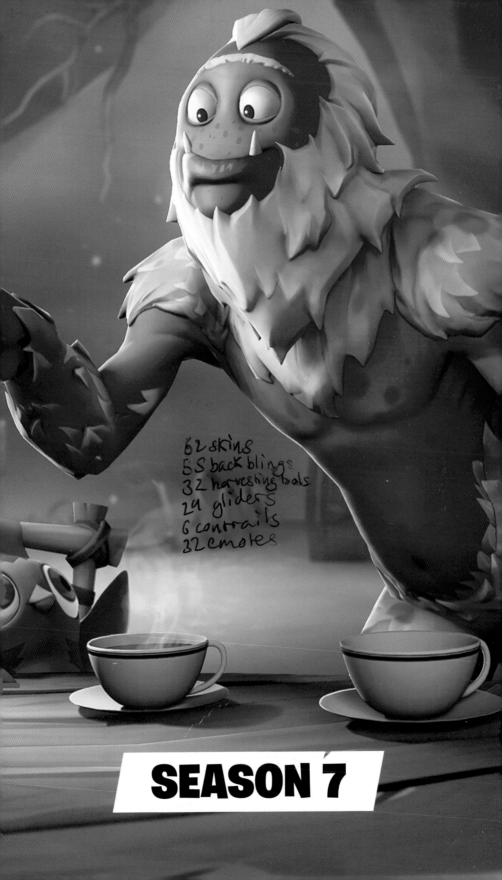

62 skins
55 back blings
32 harvesting tools
29 gliders
6 contrails
32 emotes

SEASON 7

ARK
RARITY: LEGENDARY
SET: ETERNAL STRUGGLE

CABBIE
RARITY: UNCOMMON
SET: RACER ROYALE

CLOAKED SHADOW
RARITY: EPIC

CLOUDBREAKER
RARITY: RARE
SET: AVIATION AGE

COBALT
RARITY: EPIC

CRACKABELLA
RARITY: EPIC
SET: NUTCRACKER

DEEP SEA DESTROYER
RARITY: EPIC
SET: DEEP SEA

DEEP SEA DOMINATOR
RARITY: EPIC
SET: DEEP SEA

DISCO DIVA
RARITY: RARE
SET: FORTNITE FEVER

DJ BOP
RARITY: LEGENDARY
SET: TWIN TURNTABLES

OVE RANGER
ENDARY
HEARTS

FIREWALKER
RARITY: RARE

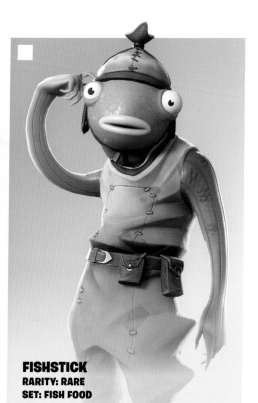

FISHSTICK
RARITY: RARE
SET: FISH FOOD

FROZEN LOVE RANGER
SERIES: FROZEN
SET: FROZEN LEGENDS

FROZEN RAVEN
SERIES: FROZEN
SET: FROZEN LEGENDS

FROZEN RED KNIGHT
SERIES: FROZEN
SET: FROZEN LEGENDS

FYRA
RARITY: EPIC
SET: PRIMAL HUNTERS

GLIMMER
RARITY: LEGENDARY
SET: WINTER WONDERLAND

GRIMBLES
RARITY: RARE

HEARTBREAKER
RARITY: RARE
SET: ROYALE HEARTS

INSIGHT
RARITY: RARE
SET: RANGED RECON

JAEGER
RARITY: EPIC
SET: PRIMAL HUNTERS

KITBASH
RARITY: EPIC
SET: BONEYARD

KRAMPUS
RARITY: LEGENDARY
SET: KRAMPUS

LACE
RARITY: EPIC
SET: OUROBOROS

LIL' WHIP
RARITY: EPIC
SET: TWO SCOOPS

LONGSHOT
RARITY: RARE
SET: RANGED RECON

LYNX
RARITY: LEGENDARY
SET: LYNX

MALCORE
RARITY: EPIC
SET: ETERNAL STRUGGLE

MAVEN
RARITY: RARE
SET: CALCULATOR CREW

ONESIE
RARITY: EPIC
SET: DURRR BURGER

PARADOX
RARITY: EPIC
SET: OUROBOROS

POWDER
RARITY: EPIC
SET: POWDER PATROL

PRODIGY
RARITY: RARE
SET: CALCULATOR CREW

REBEL
RARITY: EPIC
SET: ROBO REBELS

RED-NOSED RANGER
RARITY: UNCOMMON

REVOLT
RARITY: EPIC
SET: ROBO REBELS

SGT. WINTER
RARITY: EPIC
SET: SGT WINTER

SKULLY
RARITY: RARE
SET: SKULL & BOWS

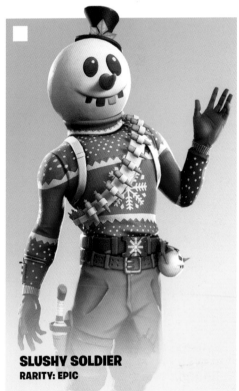

SLUSHY SOLDIER
RARITY: EPIC

SNOWFOOT
RARITY: EPIC
SET: SNOW CLAN

SNOWSTRIKE
RARITY: EPIC
SET: SNOW CLAN

SPARKPLUG
RARITY: RARE
SET: BONEYARD

SUGARPLUM
RARITY: EPIC

TECH OPS
RARITY: RARE
SET: TECH OPS

THE ICE KING
RARITY: LEGENDARY
SET: ICE KINGDOM

THE ICE QUEEN
RARITY: LEGENDARY
SET: ICE KINGDOM

THE PRISONER
RARITY: LEGENDARY

TINSELTOES
RARITY: UNCOMMON

TROG
RARITY: EPIC
SET: MOUNTAIN MYTHS

VERGE
RARITY: UNCOMMON
SET: MODERN MERCENARY

VOLLEY GIRL
RARITY: RARE

WINGTIP
RARITY: RARE
SET: AVIATION AGE

ZENITH
RARITY: LEGENDARY
SET: ZENITH

FORTNITE FACTS

THE DRAMATIC ICE KING OUTFIT COULD
BE OBTAINED AS A REWARD FOR REACHING
TIER 100 OF SEASON 7'S BATTLE PASS.

ALTITUDE
RARITY: LEGENDARY
SET: ZENITH

ARK WINGS
RARITY: LEGENDARY
SET: ETERNAL STRUGGLE

BACK PLATE
RARITY: EPIC
SET: SPANDEX SQUAD

BIRDSHOT
RARITY: LEGENDARY
SET: NUTCRACKER

BOARD BAG
RARITY: EPIC
SET: ROBO REBELS

BRAT BAG
RARITY: LEGENDARY
SET: KRAMPUS

CANNISTER CARRIER
RARITY: EPIC
SET: ROBO REBELS

CAPACITOR
RARITY: RARE
SET: TECH OPS

COMBAT WREATH
RARITY: UNCOMMON

DISCO BALL
RARITY: RARE
SET: FORTNITE FEVER

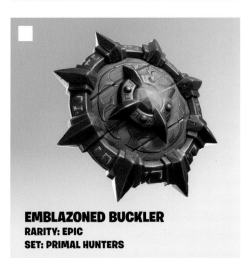

EMBLAZONED BUCKLER
RARITY: EPIC
SET: PRIMAL HUNTERS

ETERNAL
RARITY: EPIC
SET: OUROBOROS

FALLEN WINGS
RARITY: LEGENDARY
SET: ROYALE HEARTS

FLUTTERFROST
RARITY: EPIC

FROZEN IRON CAGE
SERIES: FROZEN
SET: FROZEN LEGENDS

FROZEN LOVE WINGS
SERIES: FROZEN
SET: FROZEN LEGENDS

FROZEN RED SHIELD
SERIES: FROZEN
SET: FROZEN LEGENDS

GIDDY GUNNER
RARITY: EPIC
SET: GINGERBREAD

GLIMMERING CLOAK
RARITY: LEGENDARY
SET: WINTER WONDERLAND

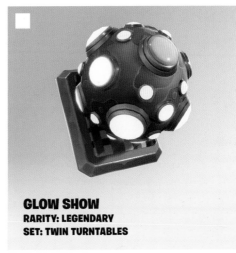

GLOW SHOW
RARITY: LEGENDARY
SET: TWIN TURNTABLES

HAMIREZ
RARITY: EPIC

ICE CUBE
RARITY: EPIC
SET: MOUNTAIN MYTHS

ICE MANTLE
RARITY: LEGENDARY
SET: ICE KINGDOM

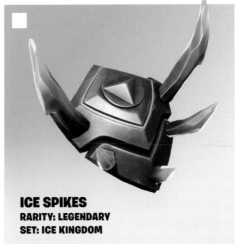

ICE SPIKES
RARITY: LEGENDARY
SET: ICE KINGDOM

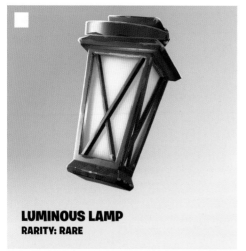

LUMINOUS LAMP
RARITY: RARE

MALCORE WINGS
RARITY: EPIC
SET: ETERNAL STRUGGLE

MERRY MUNCHKIN
RARITY: EPIC

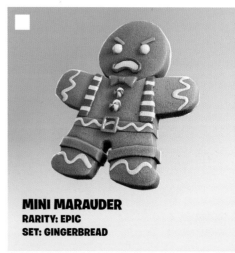

MINI MARAUDER
RARITY: EPIC
SET: GINGERBREAD

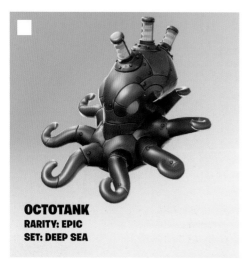

OCTOTANK
RARITY: EPIC
SET: DEEP SEA

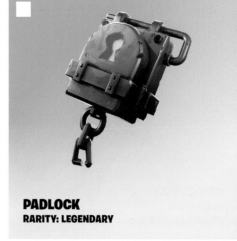

PADLOCK
RARITY: LEGENDARY

PERFECT PRESENT
RARITY: EPIC
SET: SGT. WINTER

REBREATHER
RARITY: EPIC
SET: DEEP SEA

REINFORCED BACKPLATE
RARITY: EPIC

REMUS
RARITY: EPIC

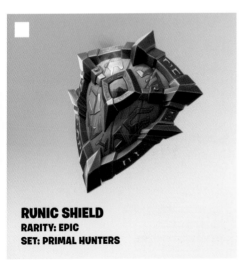

RUNIC SHIELD
RARITY: EPIC
SET: PRIMAL HUNTERS

SALTWATER SATCHEL
RARITY: RARE
SET: FISH FOOD

SCOPE SATCHEL
RARITY: RARE
SET: RANGED RECON

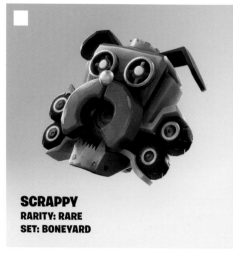

SCRAPPY
RARITY: RARE
SET: BONEYARD

SHADOW WINGS
RARITY: EPIC

SIGHT SLING
RARITY: RARE
SET: RANGED RECON

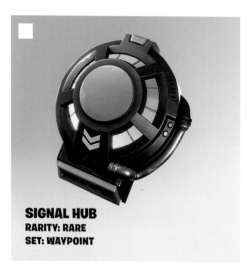

SIGNAL HUB
RARITY: RARE
SET: WAYPOINT

SKULLY SATCHEL
RARITY: RARE
SET: SKULL & BOWS

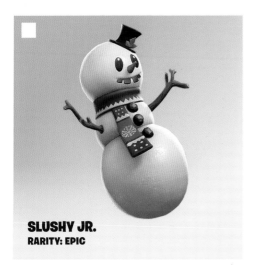

SLUSHY JR.
RARITY: EPIC

SNACKSHOT
RARITY: EPIC
SET: NUTCRACKER

SNO CONE
RARITY: EPIC
SET: TWO SCOOPS

SNOW STAR
RARITY: EPIC
SET: SNOW CLAN

SNOWBRAND
RARITY: EPIC
SET: SNOW CLAN

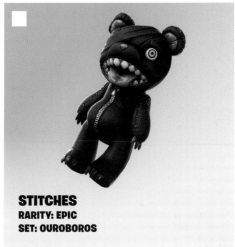

STITCHES
RARITY: EPIC
SET: OUROBOROS

SWEETHEART
RARITY: RARE
SET: ROYALE HEARTS

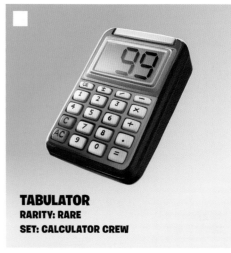

TABULATOR
RARITY: RARE
SET: CALCULATOR CREW

TECHIE
RARITY: RARE
SET: CALCULATOR CREW

TRAIL TOTE
RARITY: UNCOMMON
SET: POWDER PATROL

TRASH LID
RARITY: EPIC
SET: BONEYARD

TWISTIE INFLATOR
RARITY: RARE
SET: HOT AIR

USED RACKET
RARITY: RARE

FORTNITE FACTS
SEASON 7'S FROZEN LEGENDS PACK CONTAINED THREE FROZEN BACK BLINGS PLUS THE ACCOMPANYING OUTFITS: FROZEN RAVEN, FROZEN RED KNIGHT, AND FROZEN LOVE RANGER.

ABOMINABLE AXE
RARITY: RARE
SET: MOUNTAIN MYTHS

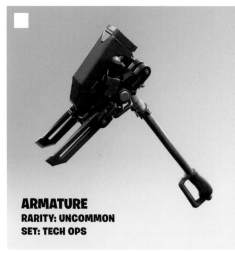

ARMATURE
RARITY: UNCOMMON
SET: TECH OPS

BATTLE AXE
RARITY: RARE
SET: PRIMAL HUNTERS

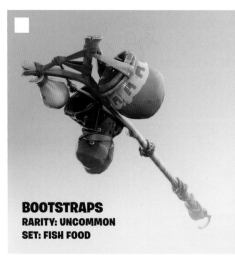

BOOTSTRAPS
RARITY: UNCOMMON
SET: FISH FOOD

BRAT CATCHER
RARITY: RARE
SET: KRAMPUS

CHOCOLLAMA
RARITY: UNCOMMON
SET: ROYALE HEARTS

CLEAN CUT
RARITY: UNCOMMON
SET: MODERN MERCENARY

COLD HEARTED
SERIES: FROZEN
SET: FROZEN LEGENDS

COLD SNAP
RARITY: RARE

COOKIE CUTTER
RARITY: UNCOMMON
SET: GINGERBREAD

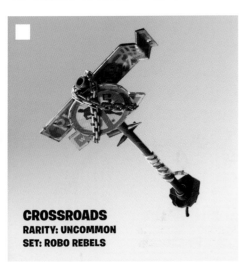

CROSSROADS
RARITY: UNCOMMON
SET: ROBO REBELS

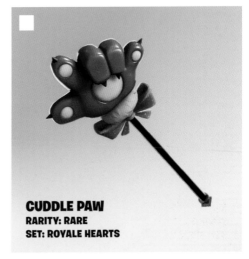

CUDDLE PAW
RARITY: RARE
SET: ROYALE HEARTS

EVIL EYE
RARITY: EPIC
SET: ETERNAL STRUGGLE

FLURRY
RARITY: RARE
SET: WINTER WONDERLAND

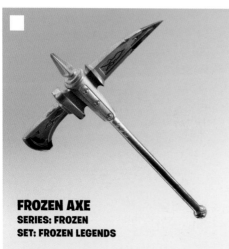

FROZEN AXE
SERIES: FROZEN
SET: FROZEN LEGENDS

FROZEN BEAK
SERIES: FROZEN
SET: FROZEN LEGENDS

ICE POP
RARITY: RARE
SET: TWO SCOOPS

ICE SCEPTER
RARITY: EPIC
SET: ICE KINGDOM

ICEBRINGER
RARITY: RARE
SET: ICE KINGDOM

ICICLE
RARITY: UNCOMMON

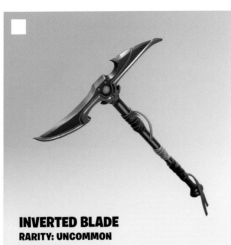

INVERTED BLADE
RARITY: UNCOMMON

KRAKENAXE
RARITY: UNCOMMON
SET: DEEP SEA

OUTBURST
RARITY: RARE

SCORCHER
RARITY: EPIC
SET: ZENITH

SEASON 7 HARVESTING TOOLS

SCRATCHMARK
RARITY: EPIC
SET: LYNX

SKULLY SPLITTER
RARITY: RARE
SET: SKULL & BOWS

SNOW GLOBE
RARITY: RARE
SET: NUTCRACKER

SQUID SRIKER
RARITY: RARE
SET: SPACE EXPLORERS

TOOTH PICK
RARITY: RARE

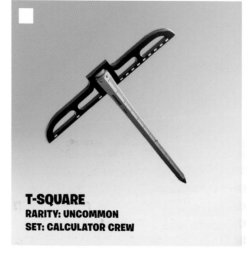

T-SQUARE
RARITY: UNCOMMON
SET: CALCULATOR CREW

VIRTUE
RARITY: RARE
SET: ETERNAL STRUGGLE

VISION
RARITY: RARE
SET: OUROBOROS

FORTNITE FACTS
THE ICE SCEPTER—WHICH COULD BE
UNLOCKED AS PART OF THE ICE KING
CHALLENGES—WAS ONE OF TEN DIFFERENT
CHILLY HARVESTING TOOLS IN THIS ICY
SEASON. CAN YOU SPOT THEM ALL? BRRR...

217

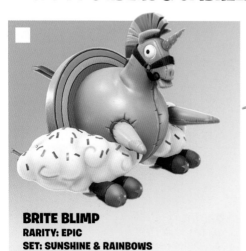

BRITE BLIMP
RARITY: EPIC
SET: SUNSHINE & RAINBOWS

COAXIAL COPTER
RARITY: EPIC
SET: TECH OPS

CORAL CRUISER
RARITY: RARE
SET: FISH FOOD

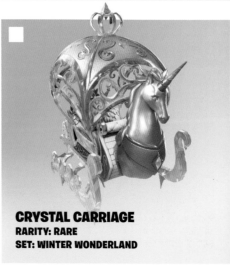

CRYSTAL CARRIAGE
RARITY: RARE
SET: WINTER WONDERLAND

DIVERGE
RARITY: RARE
SET: MODERN MERCENARY

EQUALIZER
RARITY: RARE
SET: TWIN TURNTABLES

EQUILIBRIUM
RARITY: UNCOMMON
SET: OUROBOROS

EXTRA CHEESE
RARITY: EPIC
SET: PIZZA PIT

FROZEN FEATHERS
SERIES: FROZEN
SET: FROZEN LEGENDS

GINGERSLED
RARITY: UNCOMMON
SET: GINGERBREAD

GLIDURRR
RARITY: RARE
SET: DURRR BURGER

HEARTSPAN
RARITY: RARE
SET: ROYALE HEARTS

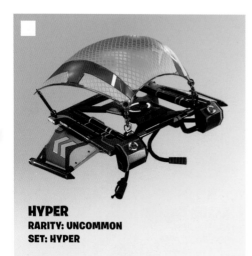

HYPER
RARITY: UNCOMMON
SET: HYPER

ICE CREAM CRUISER
RARITY: RARE
SET: TWO SCOOPS

KRAMPUS' LITTLE HELPER
RARITY: EPIC
SET: KRAMPUS

NAUTILUS
RARITY: EPIC
SET: DEEP SEA

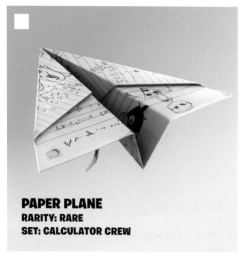

PAPER PLANE
RARITY: RARE
SET: CALCULATOR CREW

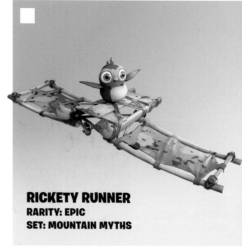

RICKETY RUNNER
RARITY: EPIC
SET: MOUNTAIN MYTHS

ROYALE AIR
RARITY: UNCOMMON
SET: POWDER PATROL

SNOWBLADES
RARITY: RARE
SET: SNOW CLAN

SNOWFALL
RARITY: COMMON

TACTICAL SLEIGH
RARITY: RARE
SET: SGT. WINTER

TUSK
RARITY: UNCOMMON
SET: PRIMAL HUNTERS

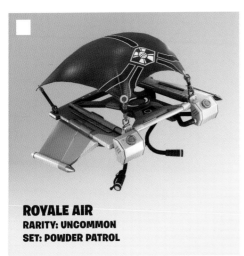

WINTER'S THORN
RARITY: RARE
SET: ICE KINGDOM

FIBER OPTICS
RARITY: RARE

GLYPHS
SERIES: DARK
SET: LIGHTNING & THUNDERSTORMS

SNOWFLAKES
RARITY: RARE

STRING LIGHTS
RARITY: RARE

SWIRLS
RARITY: RARE

VINES
RARITY: RARE

FORTNITE FACTS

GLYPHS IS THE ONLY CONTRAIL IN CHAPTER 1 TO BE PART OF THE "DARK" SERIES. IT COULD BE UNLOCKED AT TIER 37 OF THE BATTLE PASS.

ACCOLADES
RARITY: RARE

AIR HORN
RARITY: UNCOMMON

BACKSTROKE
RARITY: RARE

BOBBIN'
RARITY: RARE

CAT FLIP
RARITY: RARE
SET: LYNX

CHEER UP
RARITY: EPIC

CLEAN GROOVE
RARITY: RARE

CRACKDOWN
RARITY: EPIC

DAYDREAM
RARITY: EPIC

FLUX
RARITY: RARE

FREE FLOW
RARITY: EPIC

GET FUNKY
RARITY: RARE

GLOWSTICKS
RARITY: EPIC

GOLF CLAP
RARITY: UNCOMMON

GROUND POUND
RARITY: UNCOMMON

IDK
RARITY: UNCOMMON

JAMBOREE
RARITY: RARE

KNEE SLAPPER
RARITY: RARE

LAZY SHUFFLE
RARITY: RARE

MIC DROP
RARITY: RARE

MIME TIME
RARITY: RARE

MIND BLOWN
RARITY: UNCOMMON

OVERDRIVE
RARITY: RARE

POINT IT OUT
RARITY: RARE
SET: ICE KINGDOM

SHAOLIN SIT-UP
RARITY: UNCOMMON

SHIMMER
RARITY: RARE

SHOWSTOPPER
RARITY: RARE

SEASON 7 EMOTES

SLICK
RARITY: RARE

TAKE THE ELF
RARITY: UNCOMMON

TIME OUT
RARITY: UNCOMMON

UNWRAPPED
RARITY: UNCOMMON

WHIRLWIND
RARITY: RARE

FORTNITE FACTS
**CAT FLIP COULD BE UNLOCKED AS
PART OF THE LYNX CHALLENGES
IN THE SEASON 7 BATTLE PASS.**

SEASON 8

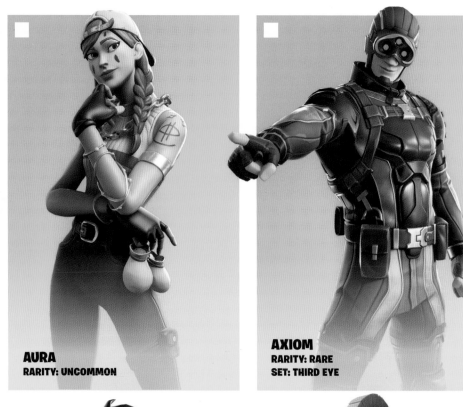

AURA
RARITY: UNCOMMON

AXIOM
RARITY: RARE
SET: THIRD EYE

BANDOLETTE
RARITY: RARE
SET: TROPIC TROOPERS

BEASTMODE (JACKAL)
RARITY: EPIC
SET: MECHANIMAL

BEASTMODE (JAGUAR)
RARITY: EPIC
SET: MECHANIMAL

BEASTMODE (LION)
RARITY: EPIC
SET: MECHANIMAL

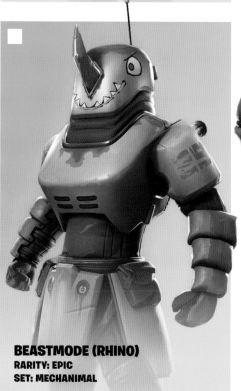

BEASTMODE (RHINO)
RARITY: EPIC
SET: MECHANIMAL

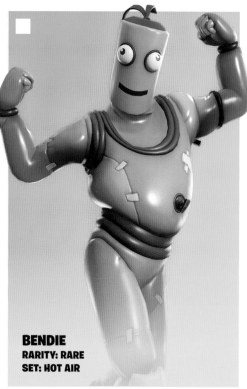

BENDIE
RARITY: RARE
SET: HOT AIR

BIRDIE
RARITY: UNCOMMON
SET: TEED OFF

BLACKHEART
RARITY: LEGENDARY
SET: SCALLYWAGS

BUCCANEER
RARITY: RARE
SET: SCALLYWAGS

CARBON COMMANDO
RARITY: RARE

COLE
RARITY: UNCOMMON

DARING DUELIST
RARITY: EPIC
SET: SCALLYWAGS

DREAM
RARITY: RARE
SET: BROKEN LIGHT

EMBER
RARITY: EPIC
SET: ASHEN GUARD

FASTBALL
RARITY: RARE
SET: THREE STRIKES

FISHSTICK (PIRATE)
RARITY: RARE
SET: FISH FOOD

GUILD
RARITY: UNCOMMON

HAYSEED
RARITY: UNCOMMON
SET: FATAL FIELDERS

HOPPER
RARITY: RARE
SET: HOPPITY HEIST

HYBRID
RARITY: LEGENDARY
SET: BROOD

HYPERNOVA
RARITY: RARE
SET: TECH OPS

INFERNO
RARITY: LEGENDARY
SET: INFERNO

INSTINCT
RARITY: RARE
SET: COUNTERATTACK

KENJI
RARITY: EPIC
SET: FALCON CLAN

KUNO
RARITY: EPIC
SET: FALCON CLAN

LAGUNA
RARITY: RARE
SET: BEACH BATTALION

LUCKY RIDER
RARITY: EPIC
SET: GREEN CLOVER

LUMINOS
RARITY: EPIC
SET: INTERSTELLAR

LUXE
RARITY: LEGENDARY
SET: 24K

MALICE
RARITY: LEGENDARY
SET: DIABOLICAL

MARINO
RARITY: RARE
SET: BEACH BATTALION

MASTER KEY
RARITY: EPIC
SET: KEY FORCE

...RE
...LDIERS

MOLTEN BATTLE HOUND
SERIES: LAVA
SET: LAVA LEGENDS

MOLTEN VALKYRIE
SERIES: LAVA
SET: LAVA LEGENDS

MUNITIONS MAJOR
RARITY: UNCOMMON

NIGHTWITCH
RARITY: EPIC
SET: MOONBONE

NITEHARE
RARITY: EPIC
SET: NITEHARE

PASTEL
RARITY: UNCOMMON
SET: PASTEL PATROL

PEELY
RARITY: EPIC
SET: BANANA BUNCH

PRICKLY PATROLLER
RARITY: UNCOMMON

PSION
RARITY: RARE
SET: THIRD EYE

RUIN
RARITY: LEGENDARY
SET: RUINATION

SEA WOLF
RARITY: RARE
SET: SCALLYWAGS

SHAMAN
RARITY: EPIC
SET: MOONBONE

SIDEWINDER
RARITY: EPIC
SET: SNAKEPIT

SLUGGER
RARITY: RARE
SET: THREE STRIKES

STEALTH REFLEX
RARITY: RARE
SET: COUNTERATTACK

STERLING
RARITY: EPIC
SET: 24K

SUNBIRD
RARITY: RARE
SET: SUN SOLDIERS

SUNFLOWER
RARITY: UNCOMMON
SET: FATAL FIELDERS

SUPERSONIC
RARITY: LEGENDARY
SET: AIR ROYALE

TWISTIE
RARITY: RARE
SET: HOT AIR

BANANA BAG
RARITY: RARE
SET: BEACH BATTALION

BARREL & BOOTY
RARITY: RARE
SET: SCALLYWAGS

BATTLE MASK
RARITY: EPIC
SET: MOONBONE

BENDIE INFLATOR
RARITY: RARE
SET: HOT AIR

BUNNY BAG
RARITY: RARE
SET: HOPPITY HEIST

CARBON PACK
RARITY: RARE

COBRA
RARITY: RARE
SET: SNAKEPIT

COMMISSION
RARITY: RARE
SET: THIRD EYE

CRYSTAL LLAMA
RARITY: RARE
SET: GETAWAY GANG

CUDDLE DOLL
RARITY: EPIC
SET: MOONBONE

DIAMOND STAR
RARITY: EPIC
SET: 24K

DODGER
RARITY: EPIC

DOUBLE PLAY
RARITY: RARE
SET: THREE STRIKES

DUAL KAMA
RARITY: EPIC
SET: FALCON CLAN

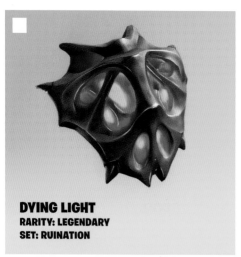

DYING LIGHT
RARITY: LEGENDARY
SET: RUINATION

EMPRESS
RARITY: EPIC

FLOPPY
RARITY: EPIC
SET: NITEHARE

GAUGE
RARITY: LEGENDARY
SET: AIR ROYALE

HAYSTACKS
RARITY: UNCOMMON
SET: FATAL FIELDERS

HIGH CALIBER
RARITY: LEGENDARY
SET: 24K

HYPNOTIC
RARITY: RARE
SET: SUN SOLDIERS

KATANA & KUNAI
RARITY: EPIC
SET: FALCON CLAN

LUCKY COINS
RARITY: UNCOMMON
SET: GREEN CLOVER

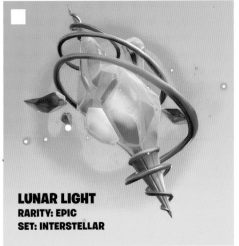

LUNAR LIGHT
RARITY: EPIC
SET: INTERSTELLAR

MALICE WINGS
RARITY: LEGENDARY
SET: DIABOLICAL

MASTER PORTAL
RARITY: EPIC
SET: KEY FORCE

MOLTEN CRESTED CAPE
SERIES: LAVA
SET: LAVA LEGENDS

MOLTEN VALKYRIE WINGS
SERIES: LAVA
SET: LAVA LEGENDS

MUTINY
RARITY: LEGENDARY
SET: SCALLYWAGS

OMISSION
RARITY: RARE
SET: THIRD EYE

OSCILLOSCOPE
RARITY: RARE
SET: TECH OPS

PINEAPPLE STRUMMER
RARITY: RARE
SET: BEACH BATTALION

RAINBOW CLOVER
RARITY: EPIC
SET: GREEN CLOVER

REACTION TANK
RARITY: RARE
SET: COUNTERATTACK

RESPONSE UNIT
RARITY: RARE
SET: COUNTERATTACK

SEAWORTHY
RARITY: RARE
SET: SCALLYWAGS

SHATTERED WING
RARITY: RARE
SET: BROKEN LIGHT

SLICE 'N DICE
RARITY: EPIC
SET: SCALLYWAGS

STEALTH RESPONSE UNIT
RARITY: RARE
SET: COUNTERATTACK

STRIKE ZONE
RARITY: RARE
SET: THREE STRIKES

SUN SPROUT
RARITY: UNCOMMON
SET: FATAL FIELDERS

SUN WINGS
RARITY: RARE
SET: SUN SOLDIERS

V6
RARITY: EPIC
SET: MECHANIMAL

VOLATILE
RARITY: EPIC
SET: SHORT FUSE

WOODSY
RARITY: EPIC

FORTNITE FACTS
SEASON 8'S BATTLE PASS ALLOWED YOU TO UNLOCK NEW STYLES FOR TWO OF THE PETS: DODGER HAD DEFAULT, BLACK, AND CAMO VARIANTS; WOODSY CAME IN DEFAULT, PIRATE, AND GOLD.

ANGULAR AXE
RARITY: UNCOMMON
SET: COUNTERATTACK

ASTRAL AXE
RARITY: EPIC
SET: INTERSTELLAR

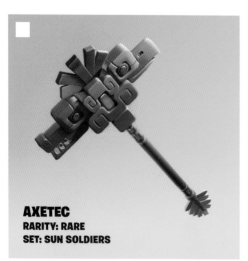

AXETEC
RARITY: RARE
SET: SUN SOLDIERS

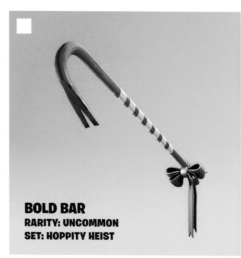

BOLD BAR
RARITY: UNCOMMON
SET: HOPPITY HEIST

BRUTE FORCE
RARITY: UNCOMMON
SET: TECH OPS

BURNING AXE
RARITY: EPIC
SET: DIABOLICAL

CRIMSON SCYTHE
RARITY: RARE
SET: INFERNO

DEMON SKULL
RARITY: EPIC

DRAGON'S CLAW
RARITY: EPIC
SET: BROOD

DREAD
RARITY: RARE
SET: RUINATION

DRIVER
RARITY: UNCOMMON
SET: TEED OFF

EMERALD SMASHER
RARITY: RARE
SET: GREEN CLOVER

FLAWLESS
RARITY: EPIC
SET: 24K

FLIMSIE FLAIL
RARITY: RARE
SET: HOT AIR

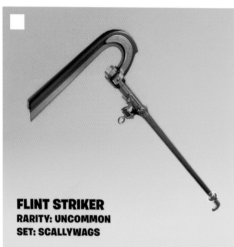

FLINT STRIKER
RARITY: UNCOMMON
SET: SCALLYWAGS

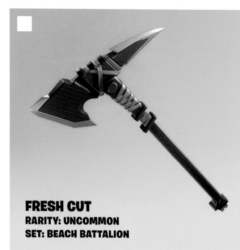

FRESH CUT
RARITY: UNCOMMON
SET: BEACH BATTALION

GOLD DIGGER
RARITY: RARE
SET: FATAL FIELDERS

GRAND SLAMMER
RARITY: UNCOMMON
SET: THREE STRIKES

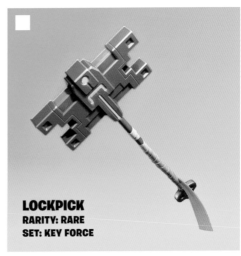

HIGH SEAS
RARITY: RARE
SET: SCALLYWAGS

LOCKPICK
RARITY: RARE
SET: KEY FORCE

MACHETE
RARITY: UNCOMMON
SET: TROPIC TROOPERS

MAULER
RARITY: EPIC
SET: MECHANIMAL

MOONBONE
RARITY: RARE
SET: MOONBONE

PEELY PICK
RARITY: RARE
SET: BANANA BUNCH

PRICKLY AXE
RARITY: RARE

PSIONIC EDGE
RARITY: RARE
SET: THIRD EYE

QUICKSTRIKE
RARITY: UNCOMMON
SET: FALCON CLAN

RELAX AXE
RARITY: RARE

ROCKBREAKER
RARITY: RARE

SHRAPNEL
RARITY: UNCOMMON
SET: SHORT FUSE

SILVER SLEDGE
RARITY: RARE
SET: 24K

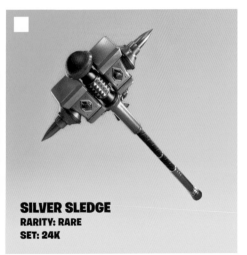

SNAKEBITE
RARITY: RARE
SET: SNAKEPIT

SPROUT
RARITY: UNCOMMON
SET: PASTEL PATROL

STAR WAND
RARITY: RARE

STEALTH ANGULAR AXE
RARITY: UNCOMMON
SET: COUNTERATTACK

STEEL CARROT
RARITY: RARE
SET: NITEHARE

STUMPY
RARITY: RARE

SWAG SMASHER
RARITY: EPIC
SET: SCALLYWAGS

TRI-STAR
RARITY: RARE

FORTNITE FACTS

THE CRIMSON SCYTHE FEATURED AS PART OF INFERNO'S
CHALLENGE PACK, WHICH ALSO CONTAINED THE INFERNO
OUTFIT, AND INFERNAL AND BURNMARK WRAPS.

ARCANA
RARITY: EPIC
SET: BROKEN LIGHT

BOOTY BUOY
RARITY: EPIC
SET: SCALLYWAGS

CHOPPA
RARITY: EPIC
SET: TROPIC TROOPERS

CINDER
RARITY: UNCOMMON
SET: ASHEN GUARD

CUDDLE CRUISER
RARITY: RARE
SET: ROYALE HEARTS

DISRUPTOR
RARITY: RARE
SET: THIRD EYE

FALCON
RARITY: LEGENDARY
SET: FALCON CLAN

FUEL
RARITY: RARE
SET: MECHANIMAL

GLOBETROTTER
RARITY: UNCOMMON

HOME RUN
RARITY: UNCOMMON
SET: THREE STRIKES

LAVAWING
RARITY: LEGENDARY
SET: LAVA LEGENDS

LOCKSTEP
RARITY: RARE
SET: KEY FORCE

PALM LEAF
RARITY: COMMON

PIVOT
RARITY: RARE
SET: COUNTERATTACK

PLUNDER
RARITY: UNCOMMON
SET: SCALLYWAGS

SKY SERPENTS
RARITY: RARE
SET: SNAKEPIT

STEALTH PIVOT
RARITY: RARE
SET: COUNTERATTACK

SUNRISE
RARITY: RARE
SET: SUN SOLDIERS

SUREFIRE
RARITY: UNCOMMON
SET: AIR ROYALE

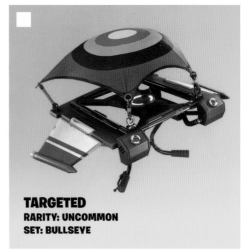

TARGETED
RARITY: UNCOMMON
SET: BULLSEYE

FORTNITE FACTS
**FUEL COMES IN FOUR DIFFERENT STYLES, TO
MATCH ITS BEASTMODE OUTFIT EQUIVALENTS:
RHINO, JACKAL, JAGUAR, AND LION.**

BALLISTICS
RARITY: RARE

CLOVERS
RARITY: RARE
SET: GREEN CLOVER

FLYING STANDARD
RARITY: RARE

LAVA
RARITY: RARE

PHANTASM
RARITY: RARE
SET: SCALLYWAGS

FORTNITE FACTS
TO UNLOCK THE BALLISTICS CONTRAIL, YOU'D HAVE TO REACH TIER 85 OF THE BATTLE PASS.

BOOBYTRAPPED
RARITY: EPIC

BREEZY
RARITY: UNCOMMON
SET: HOT AIR

BUNNY HOP
RARITY: RARE

CONGA
RARITY: RARE

DRAGON STANCE
RARITY: RARE
SET: BROOD

DREAM FEET
RARITY: RARE

DRUM MAJOR
RARITY: RARE

FANCIFUL
RARITY: RARE

FANDANGLE
RARITY: RARE

FIERCE
RARITY: RARE
SET: 24K

FIRE SPINNER
RARITY: EPIC

HELLO FRIEND
RARITY: UNCOMMON

HOOP MASTER
RARITY: EPIC

JAZZ HANDS
RARITY: UNCOMMON

LAVISH
RARITY: RARE

NANA NANA
RARITY: RARE

PUNCHED UP
RARITY: UNCOMMON

RAINING DOUBLOONS
RARITY: RARE

SHADOW BOXER
RARITY: UNCOMMON

SLAP HAPPY
RARITY: RARE

SNOOZEFEST
RARITY: RARE

SPRING-LOADED
RARITY: RARE

SPYGLASS
RARITY: RARE

SWITCHSTEP
RARITY: RARE

FORTNITE FACTS
DRAGON STANCE COULD BE OBTAINED AS PART OF THE HYBRID CHALLENGES, EXCLUSIVE TO THE SEASON 8 BATTLE PASS.

68. 80%
4 sboard
29 whoops
22 gloves
8 con rats
36 emote

SEASON 9

ANARCHY AGENT
RARITY: UNCOMMON
SET: ANARCHY

ASMODEUS
RARITY: RARE
SET: BATTLE RITES

BACHII
RARITY: RARE
SET: BATTLE BUN

BANNER TROOPER
RARITY: UNCOMMON
SET: BANNER BRIGADE

BEACH BOMBER
RARITY: RARE
SET: SUNSHINE & RAINBOWS

BIGFOOT
RARITY: RARE
SET: BIGFOOT

BIZ
RARITY: RARE
SET: ROUGHNECK

BOLT
RARITY: UNCOMMON

271

BRACER
RARITY: UNCOMMON

BRANDED BRAWLER
RARITY: UNCOMMON
SET: BANNER BRIGADE

BRANDED BRIGADIER
RARITY: UNCOMMON
SET: BANNER BRIGADE

BREAKPOINT
RARITY: RARE
SET: WAYPOINT

BUNKER JONESY
RARITY: EPIC
SET: BUNKER DAYS

CALLISTO
RARITY: RARE
SET: BATTLE RITES

COPPER WASP
RARITY: EPIC
SET: KATA TECH

CRYPTIC
RARITY: RARE
SET: CRYPTIC

DARE
RARITY: RARE

DARK VERTEX
RARITY: LEGENDARY
SET: DARK APEX

DEMI
RARITY: EPIC
SET: SCARLET DRAGON

DESERT DOMINATOR
RARITY: UNCOMMON

DOGGO
RARITY: EPIC
SET: GRUMBLE GANG

DOUBLECROSS
RARITY: RARE
SET: RED LILY

ETHER
RARITY: EPIC
SET: NEOCHASER

FISHSTICK (VR)
RARITY: RARE
SET: FISH FOOD

FISHSTICK (WORLD CUP)
RARITY: RARE
SET: FISH FOOD

FLARE
RARITY: EPIC
SET: STORMLIGHT

FLUTTER
RARITY: RARE
SET: CHRYSALIS CREW

FOCUS
RARITY: RARE
SET: FOCAL POINT

GAGE
RARITY: UNCOMMON

HEIST
RARITY: RARE
SET: GETAWAY GANG

KING FLAMINGO
RARITY: UNCOMMON
SET: FLAMINGO

LT. LOGO
RARITY: UNCOMMON
SET: BANNER BRIGADE

SEASON 9 OUTFITS

MARKED MARAUDER
RARITY: UNCOMMON
SET: BANNER BRIGADE

MATCH POINT
RARITY: UNCOMMON

MECHA TEAM LEADER
RARITY: EPIC
SET: FINAL SHOWDOWN

MIKA
RARITY: RARE

NEO VERSA
RARITY: EPIC
SET: NEOCHASER

NITEBEAM
RARITY: EPIC
SET: STORMLIGHT

PERFECT SHADOW
SERIES: SHADOW

PILLAR
RARITY: RARE
SET: CHRYSALIS CREW

PLASTIC PATROLLER
RARITY: UNCOMMON
SET: TOY SOLDIER

RELAY
RARITY: UNCOMMON

ROX
RARITY: LEGENDARY
SET: SKY STYLE

SANDSTORM
RARITY: RARE
SET: IMMORTAL SANDS

SCIMITAR
RARITY: RARE
SET: IMMORTAL SANDS

SENTINEL
RARITY: LEGENDARY
SET: BATTLE DYNAMICS

SGT. SIGIL
RARITY: UNCOMMON
SET: BANNER BRIGADE

SHADOW SKULLY
SERIES: SHADOW
SET: SKULL & BOWS

SHADOWBIRD
SERIES: SHADOW
SET: SUN SOLDIERS

SIGNATURE SNIPER
RARITY: UNCOMMON
SET: BANNER BRIGADE

SINGULARITY
RARITY: LEGENDARY

STARFISH
RARITY: EPIC
SET: FISH FOOD

STRATUS
RARITY: EPIC
SET: STORM STALKER

SUMMER DRIFT
RARITY: EPIC
SET: DRIFT

SYMBOL STALWART
RARITY: UNCOMMON
SET: BANNER BRIGADE

SYNAPSE
RARITY: EPIC
SET: SYNAPSE

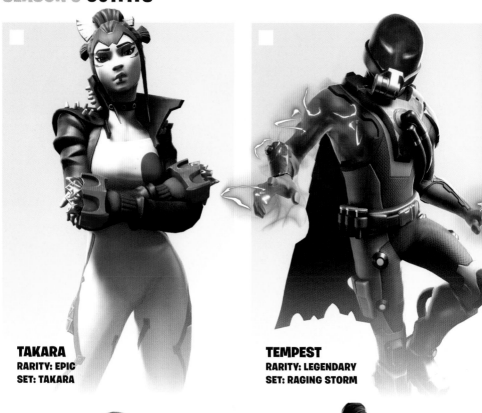

TAKARA
RARITY: EPIC
SET: TAKARA

TEMPEST
RARITY: LEGENDARY
SET: RAGING STORM

TOY TROOPER
RARITY: UNCOMMON
SET: TOY SOLDIER

TSUKI
RARITY: RARE
SET: KATA TECH

VECTOR
RARITY: RARE
SET: TOTAL CONTROL

VEGA
RARITY: EPIC
SET: BOUNTY HUNTER

VELOCITY
RARITY: LEGENDARY

VENDETTA
RARITY: LEGENDARY
SET: SUIT UP

VERSA
RARITY: EPIC
SET: NEOCHASER

WILDE
RARITY: EPIC
SET: WHITE TIGER

WONDER
RARITY: EPIC

WORLD WARRIOR
SET: WORLD CUP 2019
RARITY: UNCOMMON

FORTNITE FACTS

THE ROX OUTFIT WAS THE TIER 1 REWARD FOR SEASON 9'S BATTLE PASS. THIS HIGHLY CUSTOMIZABLE SKIN HAS FIVE DIFFERENT STAGES, THREE CLOTHING COLORS, AND EVEN THREE ACCESSORY COLORS.

ANEMONE
RARITY: EPIC
SET: FISH FOOD

BACK BOARD
RARITY: EPIC
SET: HANG TIME

BACKTRACKER
RARITY: EPIC
SET: STORM STALKER

BANNER CAPE
RARITY: RARE
SET: BANNER BRIGADE

BRAVE BAG
RARITY: UNCOMMON
SET: STARS & STRIPES

BRITE BOARD
RARITY: RARE
SET: SUNSHINE & RAINBOWS

CARAPACE
RARITY: RARE
SET: CHRYSALIS CREW

CHOW DOWN
RARITY: EPIC
SET: GRUMBLE GANG

CHUCK PACK
RARITY: RARE
SET: FOCAL POINT

CNXN
RARITY: EPIC
SET: NEOCHASER

COLOR GUARD
RARITY: UNCOMMON
SET: STARS & STRIPES

COOLER
RARITY: RARE
SET: BIGFOOT

DARK DEFLECTOR
RARITY: LEGENDARY
SET: DARK APEX

FLORAL SHELL
RARITY: RARE
SET: RED LILY

FLUTTER WINGS
RARITY: RARE
SET: CHRYSALIS CREW

GAZE
RARITY: EPIC
SET: TAKARA

GLOW JET
RARITY: RARE
SET: ROUGHNECK

GO BAG
RARITY: EPIC
SET: BOUNTY HUNTER

HEXXED
RARITY: RARE
SET: BATTLE RITES

HOLO-PACK
RARITY: EPIC
SET: SYNAPSE

HOT WING
RARITY: LEGENDARY
SET: BATTLE DYNAMICS

JET SET
RARITY: EPIC
SET: FINAL SHOWDOWN

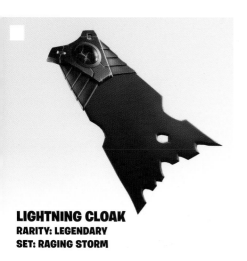

LIGHTNING CLOAK
RARITY: LEGENDARY
SET: RAGING STORM

LUMI CORE GREEN
RARITY: EPIC
SET: STORMLIGHT

LUMI CORE RED
RARITY: EPIC
SET: STORMLIGHT

MOCHI
RARITY: RARE
SET: BATTLE BUN

NANA CAPE
RARITY: EPIC
SET: BUNKER DAYS

NEO PHRENZY
RARITY: EPIC
SET: NEOCHASER

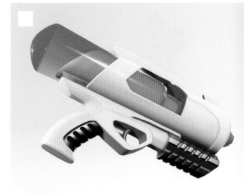

OCULAR
RARITY: RARE
SET: BATTLE RITES

OOZIE
RARITY: EPIC
SET: DRIFT

PALETTE PACK
RARITY: EPIC
SET: WHITE TIGER

PERFECT WINGS
SERIES: SHADOW

PHRENZY
RARITY: EPIC
SET: NEOCHASER

QUACK PACK
RARITY: UNCOMMON

RETRIBUTION
RARITY: LEGENDARY
SET: SUIT UP

SCARLET EDGE
RARITY: EPIC
SET: SCARLET DRAGON

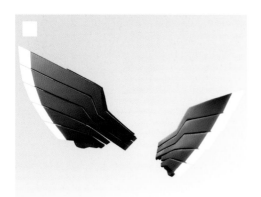

SHADOWBIRD WINGS
SERIES: SHADOW
SET: SUN SOLDIERS

SIGNAL JAMMER
RARITY: RARE
SET: WAYPOINT

SMOOTHIE
RARITY: RARE
SET: BUNKER DAYS

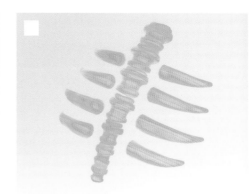

SPECTRAL SPINE
RARITY: RARE
SET: CRYPTIC

STARK SATCHEL
SERIES: SHADOW
SET: SKULL & BOWS

STREAMLINE
RARITY: RARE

STRIPED STALKER
RARITY: EPIC
SET: KATA TECH

TAHNA
RARITY: RARE
SET: KATA TECH

TINY TOTEM
RARITY: RARE
SET: GETAWAY GANG

FORTNITE FACTS

NANA CAPE COULD BE WON AS PART OF SEASON 9'S BATTLE PASS, ALONG WITH THE RIPE RIPPERS HARVESTING TOOL—THE FIRST TO FEATURE DUAL-WIELD TECHNOLOGY.

BIRTHDAY SLICE
RARITY: UNCOMMON
SET: B-DAY BUNCH

BUNKER BASHER
RARITY: RARE
SET: BUNKER DAYS

CHEW TOY
RARITY: UNCOMMON
SET: GRUMBLE GANG

COMBO CLEAVER
RARITY: RARE
SET: FINAL SHOWDOWN

CONCH CLEAVER
RARITY: EPIC
SET: FISH FOOD

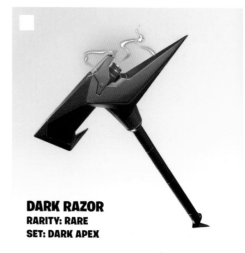

DARK RAZOR
RARITY: RARE
SET: DARK APEX

DUAL EDGE
RARITY: EPIC
SET: DRIFT

EMBLEMATIC
RARITY: UNCOMMON
SET: BANNER BRIGADE

FIXATION
RARITY: RARE
SET: FOCAL POINT

FLYCATCHER
RARITY: UNCOMMON
SET: CHRYSALIS CREW

FORK KNIFE
RARITY: UNCOMMON

FOUL PLAY
RARITY: RARE
SET: BATTLE RITES

HARMONIC AXES
RARITY: EPIC
SET: SKY STYLE

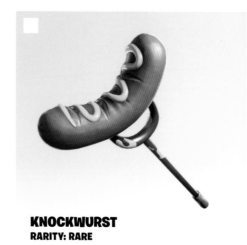

KNOCKWURST
RARITY: RARE

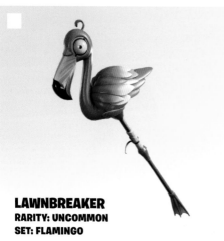

LAWNBREAKER
RARITY: UNCOMMON
SET: FLAMINGO

LOW 'N SLOW
RARITY: RARE

MECH AXE
RARITY: EPIC
SET: SUIT UP

REVOKER
RARITY: RARE
SET: BOUNTY HUNTER

RIPE RIPPERS
RARITY: RARE
SET: BUNKER DAYS

SCARLET SCYTHE
RARITY: RARE
SET: SCARLET DRAGON

SHAMISEN
RARITY: RARE
SET: TAKARA

SPLINTERED LIGHT
RARITY: RARE
SET: STORMLIGHT

STARK SPLITTER
SERIES: SHADOW
SET: SKULL & BOWS

STORM BOLT
RARITY: EPIC
SET: RAGING STORM

TALONS
RARITY: RARE
SET: FALCON CLAN

VIVID AXE
RARITY: UNCOMMON
SET: STORMLIGHT

VOX
RARITY: EPIC
SET: SKY STYLE

WEB WRECKER
RARITY: RARE
SET: NEOCHASER

WILD TANGENT
RARITY: UNCOMMON
SET: TOTAL CONTROL

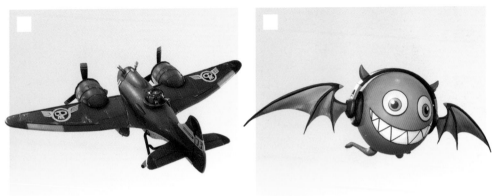

ASSAULT BOMBER
RARITY: EPIC

BATSO
RARITY: RARE
SET: BATTLE RITES

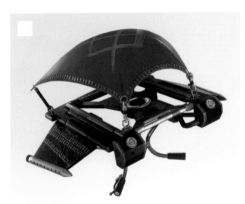

CAMP CRUISER
RARITY: RARE
SET: BIGFOOT

CHAOS
RARITY: UNCOMMON
SET: ANARCHY

CROP DUSTER
RARITY: RARE
SET: FATAL FIELDERS

COAXIAL BLUE
RARITY: EPIC

CUSTOM CRUISER
RARITY: UNCOMMON
SET: BANNER BRIGADE

DARK FORERUNNER
RARITY: EPIC
SET: DARK APEX

DRIFTSTREAM
RARITY: RARE
SET: DRIFT

ENGAGE
RARITY: UNCOMMON
SET: TAKARA

FIELD FLYER
RARITY: UNCOMMON
SET: ADVANCED FORCES

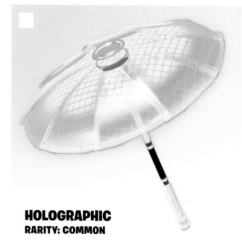

HOLOGRAPHIC
RARITY: COMMON

ION
RARITY: RARE
SET: TOTAL CONTROL

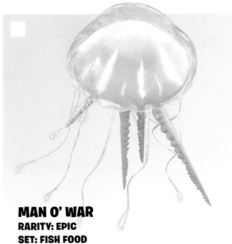

MAN O' WAR
RARITY: EPIC
SET: FISH FOOD

MEGABAT
RARITY: RARE
SET: STORMLIGHT

PAYLOAD
RARITY: UNCOMMON
SET: SUNSHINE & RAINBOWS

RETALIATOR
RARITY: RARE
SET: SUIT UP

SCARLET STRIKE
RARITY: UNCOMMON
SET: SCARLET DRAGON

STORM EYE
RARITY: EPIC
SET: RAGING STORM

TAILWIND TWISTER
RARITY: UNCOMMON
SET: STORM STALKER

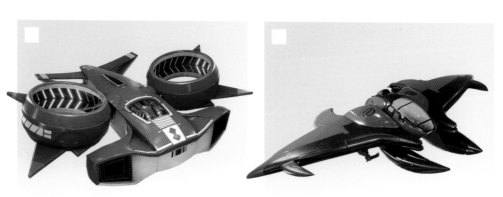

TECH TURBINE
RARITY: RARE
SET: NEOCHASER

TURBO SPIN
RARITY: EPIC
SET: SKY STYLE

FORTNITE FACTS
MAN O' WAR JOINS CORAL CRUISER (SEASON 7) IN THE FISH FOOD SET TO FORM TWO OF THE MOST UNUSUAL GLIDERS IN FORTNITE.

BANANAS!
RARITY: RARE
SET: BANANA BUNCH

BEACHBALLS
RARITY: RARE

BLUE FUSION
RARITY: RARE

CHRONO
RARITY: RARE
SET: IMMORTAL SANDS

LIGHTNING STRIKE
RARITY: RARE
SET: STORM STALKER

NEO TUBES
RARITY: RARE

PLASMA TRAIL
RARITY: RARE
SET: SUIT UP

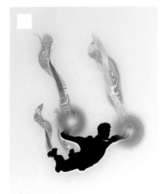

VIBRANT
RARITY: RARE

BILLY BOUNCE
RARITY: RARE

BOUNCER
RARITY: RARE

BUCKETS
RARITY: UNCOMMON
SET: HANG TIME

BUSINESS HIPS
RARITY: RARE

CARTWHEELIN'
RARITY: RARE

CLUCK STRUT
RARITY: RARE

CRABBY
RARITY: RARE

DEEP DAB
RARITY: UNCOMMON

DEEP END
RARITY: RARE

EXTRATERRESTRIAL
RARITY: RARE

FLEX ON 'EM
RARITY: UNCOMMON
SET: HANG TIME

GLITTER
RARITY: RARE

GUITAR WALK
RARITY: RARE

HANG LOOSE
RARITY: UNCOMMON

JUMP JETS
RARITY: RARE
SET: BATTLE DYNAMICS

JUMPING JACKS
RARITY: UNCOMMON

KISS THE CUP
RARITY: UNCOMMON

LAID BACK SHUFFLE
RARITY: RARE

LOCK IT UP
RARITY: UNCOMMON

MAKE IT PLANTAIN
RARITY: RARE

NO SWEAT
RARITY: RARE
SET: FINAL SHOWDOWN

OLD SCHOOL
RARITY: RARE

PEACE OUT
RARITY: UNCOMMON
SET: SKY STYLE

PICK IT UP
RARITY: RARE

PRICKLY POSE
RARITY: UNCOMMON

REVEL
RARITY: UNCOMMON

SAD TROMBONE
RARITY: RARE

SAVOR THE W
RARITY: RARE

SIGN SPINNER
RARITY: EPIC

SIGNATURE SHUFFLE
RARITY: EPIC

SIZZLIN'
RARITY: EPIC

TEAM MECH
RARITY: UNCOMMON
SET: FINAL SHOWDOWN

TEAM MONSTER
RARITY: UNCOMMON
SET: FINAL SHOWDOWN

TURBOCHARGED
RARITY: EPIC
SET: FINAL SHOWDOWN

WORK IT
RARITY: RARE

YAY!
RARITY: UNCOMMON

12 skins
47 backblings
38 harvesting tools
13 gliders
5 contrails
33 emotes

SEASON X

AERONAUT
RARITY: RARE
SET: SKY STALKER

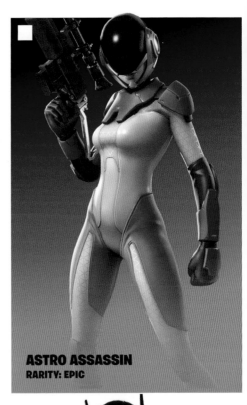

ASTRO ASSASSIN
RARITY: EPIC

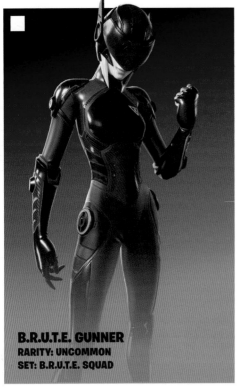

B.R.U.T.E. GUNNER
RARITY: UNCOMMON
SET: B.R.U.T.E. SQUAD

B.R.U.T.E. NAVIGATOR
RARITY: UNCOMMON
SET: B.R.U.T.E. SQUAD

BONE WASP
RARITY: EPIC
SET: STING

BRAVO LEADER
RARITY: RARE
SET: WAYPOINT

BRONTO
RARITY: RARE
SET: DINO GUARD

BUBBLE BOMBER
RARITY: RARE
SET: BUBBLEGUM

CATALYST
RARITY: LEGENDARY
SET: DRIFT

CATASTROPHE
RARITY: RARE
SET: HAZCAT

ED VOYAGER
XPLORERS

CRYSTAL
RARITY: UNCOMMON

DANGER ZONE
RARITY: RARE
SET: ZONE WARS

DARK JONESY
SERIES: DARK

DARK RED KNIGHT
SERIES: DARK
SET: FORT KNIGHTS

DARK WILD CARD
SERIES: DARK
SET: GETAWAY GANG

DEADFALL
RARITY: UNCOMMON
SET: SIEGE STRIKE

ETERNAL VOYAGER
RARITY: EPIC
SET: SPACE EXPLORERS

FACET
RITY: RARE

FENNIX
RARITY: RARE
SET: FUR FORCE

FREESTYLE
RARITY: EPIC

FRONTIER
RARITY: RARE
SET: WESTERN WILDS

GLOW
RARITY: LEGENDARY
SET: OVERSEER

GRIT
RARITY: UNCOMMON

GUACO
RARITY: RARE
SET: THE LEFTOVERS

GUTBOMB
RARITY: EPIC
SET: THE LEFTOVERS

HARD CHARGER
RARITY: UNCOMMON
SET: RPM

HOT ZONE
RARITY: RARE
SET: ZONE WARS

HOTHOUSE
RARITY: EPIC
SET: THE LEFTOVERS

HOTWIRE
RARITY: EPIC
SET: WILD SHOCK

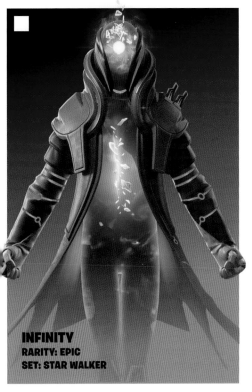

INFINITY
RARITY: EPIC
SET: STAR WALKER

KNOCKOUT
RARITY: UNCOMMON
SET: SIEGE STRIKE

LIMELIGHT
RARITY: RARE
SET: CITRON

MOXIE
RARITY: RARE
SET: TKO

OPPRESSOR
RARITY: LEGENDARY
SET: DOMINATION

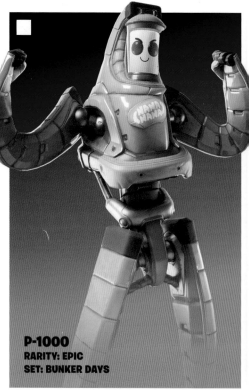

P-1000
RARITY: EPIC
SET: BUNKER DAYS

PAYBACK
RARITY: RARE
SET: RPM

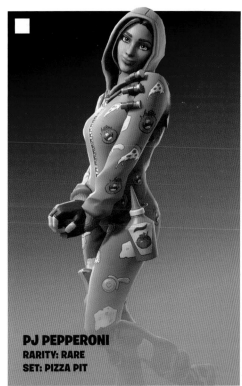

PJ PEPPERONI
RARITY: RARE
SET: PIZZA PIT

RAGSY
RARITY: EPIC
SET: THE LEFTOVERS

RECON RANGER
RARITY: UNCOMMON
SET: ADVANCED FORCES

RED STRIKE
RARITY: EPIC
SET: GOLD MASK

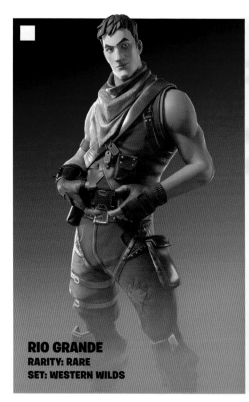

RIO GRANDE
RARITY: RARE
SET: WESTERN WILDS

ROGUE SPIDER KNIGHT
RARITY: LEGENDARY
SET: ARACHNID

SHOT CALLER
RARITY: RARE
SET: METRO SQUAD

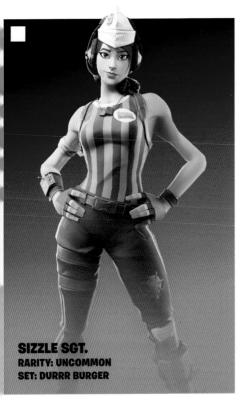

SIZZLE SGT.
RARITY: UNCOMMON
SET: DURRR BURGER

SLEDGE
RARITY: RARE
SET: HEAVY HITTER

SLINGSHOT
RARITY: UNCOMMON
SET: RACER ROYALE

SLUMBER
RARITY: EPIC
SET: DREAMY DAYS

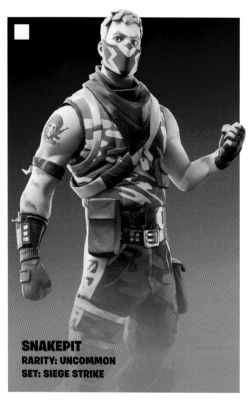

SNAKEPIT
RARITY: UNCOMMON
SET: SIEGE STRIKE

SPARKLE SUPREME
RARITY: EPIC
SET: FORTNITE FEVER

STARLIE
RARITY: RARE

STONEHEART
RARITY: EPIC
SET: ROYALE HEARTS

STREET STRIKER
RARITY: RARE

SURESHOT
RARITY: UNCOMMON

SWAMP STALKER
RARITY: UNCOMMON

THE SCIENTIST
RARITY: LEGENDARY
SET: THE SEVEN

TILTED TEKNIQUE
RARITY: EPIC
SET: AEROSOL ASSASSINS

TOXIC TAGGER
RARITY: RARE

ULTIMA KNIGHT
RARITY: LEGENDARY
SET: FORT KNIGHTS

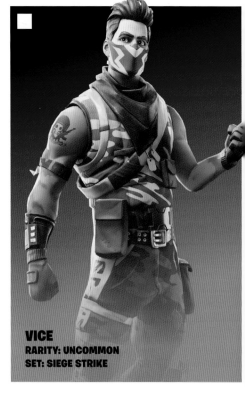

VICE
RARITY: UNCOMMON
SET: SIEGE STRIKE

VULTURE
RARITY: EPIC
SET: AIR STRIKE

X-LORD
RARITY: EPIC
SET: STORM SCAVENGER

YOND3R
RARITY: EPIC
SET: TWIN TURNTABLES

ZORGOTON
RARITY: RARE
SET: UFO

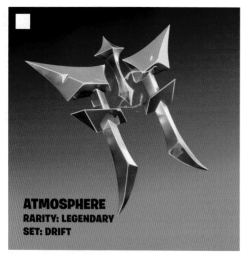

ATMOSPHERE
RARITY: LEGENDARY
SET: DRIFT

BACKBEAT
RARITY: EPIC

BANNER SHIELD
RARITY: RARE
SET: BANNER BRIGADE

BLADED BAG
RARITY: EPIC
SET: GOLD MASK

BRONTO BAG
RARITY: RARE
SET: DINO GUARD

BUBBLE BLAST
RARITY: RARE
SET: BUBBLEGUM

CHEESY
RARITY: RARE
SET: PIZZA PIT

CONTAINMENT PACK
RARITY: EPIC
SET: AIR STRIKE

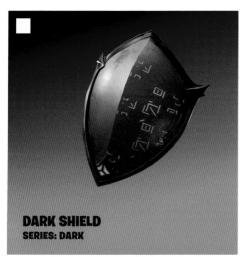

DARK SHIELD
SERIES: DARK

DETONATOR
RARITY: RARE
SET: WESTERN WILDS

DRAGONCREST
RARITY: LEGENDARY
SET: FORT KNIGHTS

DREAMER
RARITY: EPIC
SET: DREAMY DAYS

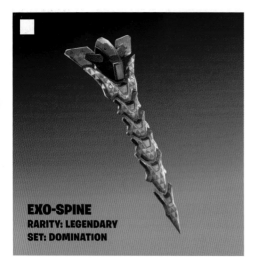

EXO-SPINE
RARITY: LEGENDARY
SET: DOMINATION

GAMEPLAN
RARITY: EPIC
SET: SPACE EXPLORERS

GEODE
RARITY: RARE

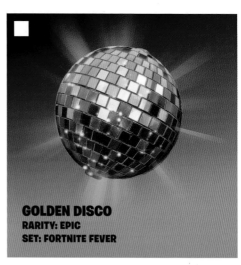

GOLDEN DISCO
RARITY: EPIC
SET: FORTNITE FEVER

GRANDE PACK
RARITY: RARE
SET: WESTERN WILDS

HEARTLESS
RARITY: EPIC
SET: THE LEFTOVERS

KITSUNE
RARITY: EPIC
SET: DRIFT

MOOSE
RARITY: RARE
SET: TKO

MOTOCASE
RARITY: UNCOMMON
SET: RPM

PAINT PACK
RARITY: EPIC
SET: AEROSOL ASSASSINS

PRIMAL DANGER
RARITY: EPIC
SET: STING

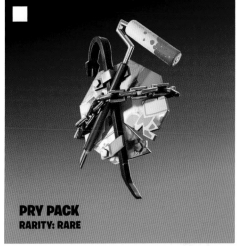

PRY PACK
RARITY: RARE

RED ALERT
RARITY: RARE
SET: STREET STRIPES

RIFT ROCK
RARITY: RARE

ROGUE SPIDER SHIELD
RARITY: LEGENDARY
SET: ARACHNID

SPIKED SATCHEL
RARITY: RARE
SET: STORM SCAVENGER

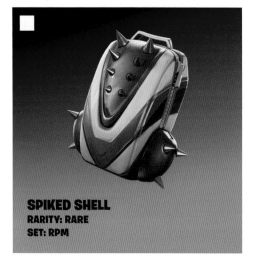

SPIKED SHELL
RARITY: RARE
SET: RPM

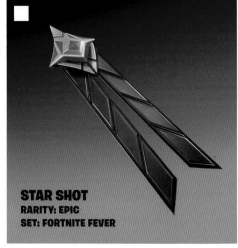

STAR SHOT
RARITY: EPIC
SET: FORTNITE FEVER

STAR SURGE
RARITY: LEGENDARY
SET: THE SEVEN

STARCREST FLUX
RARITY: RARE
SET: ZONE WARS

STARCREST SHIFT
RARITY: RARE
SET: ZONE WARS

STARFIELD
RARITY: EPIC
SET: STAR WALKER

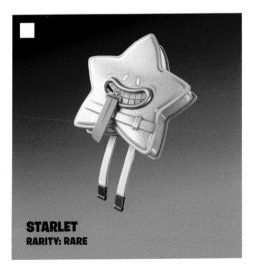

STARLET
RARITY: RARE

STRONGHOLD
RARITY: RARE
SET: HEAVY HITTER

TAKEOUT
RARITY: EPIC
SET: THE LEFTOVERS

TOMCOM
RARITY: EPIC
SET: THE LEFTOVERS

TOXIC KITTY
RARITY: RARE
SET: HAZCAT

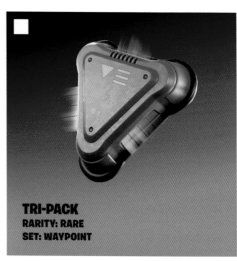

TRI-PACK
RARITY: RARE
SET: WAYPOINT

TROPHY SACK
RARITY: EPIC
SET: STORM SCAVENGER

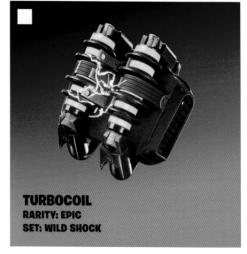

TURBOCOIL
RARITY: EPIC
SET: WILD SHOCK

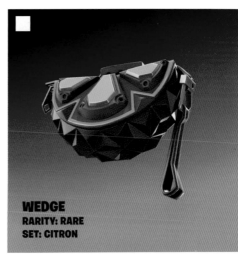

UTILITY PACK
RARITY: RARE
SET: METRO SQUAD

WEDGE
RARITY: RARE
SET: CITRON

WILD CUBE
SERIES: DARK

WINGS OF LOVE
RARITY: EPIC
SET: ROYALE HEARTS

XENOPOD
RARITY: EPIC
SET: SPACE EXPLORERS

AERO AXE
RARITY: UNCOMMON
SET: SKY STALKER

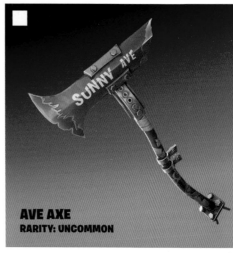

AVE AXE
RARITY: UNCOMMON

BLUE BOLT
RARITY: RARE
SET: AIR STRIKE

BUBBLE POPPER
RARITY: RARE
SET: BUBBLEGUM

CHAINED CLEAVER
RARITY: RARE
SET: RPM

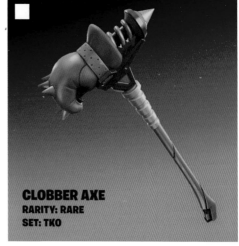

CLOBBER AXE
RARITY: RARE
SET: TKO

COSMIC CLEAVERS
RARITY: RARE
SET: SPACE EXPLORERS

CUPID'S DAGGER
RARITY: RARE
SET: ROYALE HEARTS

DARK AXE
SERIES: DARK

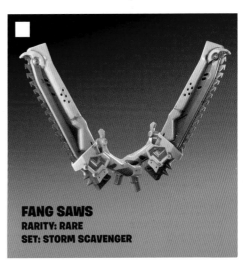

FANG SAWS
RARITY: RARE
SET: STORM SCAVENGER

FLYING SLASHER
RARITY: UNCOMMON
SET: UFO

GRILLCOUNT
RARITY: RARE
SET: THE LEFTOVERS

HYPER EDGE
RARITY: RARE
SET: ZONE WARS

IMPACT EDGE
RARITY: UNCOMMON
SET: HEAVY HITTER

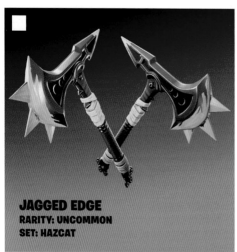

JAGGED EDGE
RARITY: UNCOMMON
SET: HAZCAT

LONGHORN
RARITY: RARE
SET: WESTERN WILDS

MEGAVOLT
RARITY: RARE
SET: WILD SHOCK

METRO MACHETES
RARITY: RARE
SET: METRO SQUAD

NIGHTY NIGHT
RARITY: RARE
SET: DREAMY DAYS

PAIR-PERONNI
RARITY: UNCOMMON
SET: PIZZA PIT

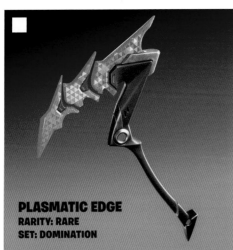

PLASMATIC EDGE
RARITY: RARE
SET: DOMINATION

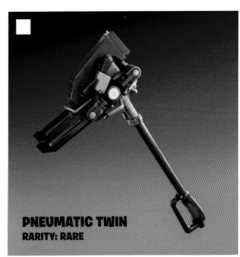

PNEUMATIC TWIN
RARITY: RARE

POWER PUNCH
RARITY: EPIC
SET: KATA TECH

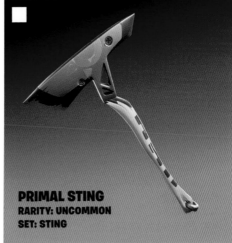

PRIMAL STING
RARITY: UNCOMMON
SET: STING

RED STREAK
RARITY: UNCOMMON
SET: GOLD MASK

RENEGADE ROLLERS
RARITY: RARE
SET: AEROSOL ASSASSINS

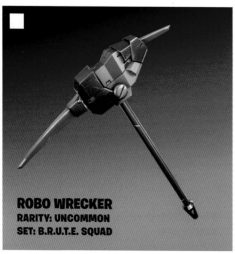

ROBO WRECKER
RARITY: UNCOMMON
SET: B.R.U.T.E. SQUAD

RUSTY ROLLER
RARITY: RARE
SET: THE LEFTOVERS

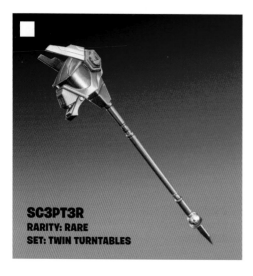

SC3PT3R
RARITY: RARE
SET: TWIN TURNTABLES

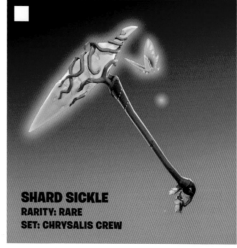

SHARD SICKLE
RARITY: RARE
SET: CHRYSALIS CREW

SNACK ATTACKERS
RARITY: RARE
SET: THE LEFTOVERS

SOUR STRIKERS
RARITY: RARE
SET: CITRON

SPARKLE SCYTHE
RARITY: RARE
SET: FORTNITE FEVER

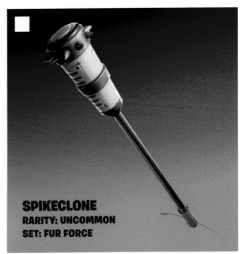

SPIKECLONE
RARITY: UNCOMMON
SET: FUR FORCE

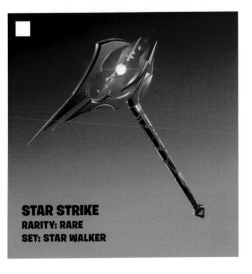

STAR STRIKE
RARITY: RARE
SET: STAR WALKER

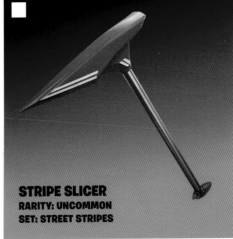

STRIPE SLICER
RARITY: UNCOMMON
SET: STREET STRIPES

TAC BATS
RARITY: UNCOMMON
SET: WAYPOINT

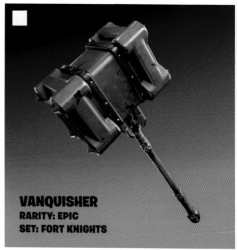

VANQUISHER
RARITY: EPIC
SET: FORT KNIGHTS

FORTNITE FACTS

PLAYING HAVOC WITH SPELLCHECK EVERYWHERE, SC3PT3R COULD BE WON BY COMPLETING ALL SEVEN BOOGIE DOWN CHALLENGES. IT IS PART OF THE LARGE TWIN TURNTABLES SET, WHICH INCLUDES THE YOND3R OUTFIT FROM SEASON X'S BATTLE PASS, AMONG OTHERS.

DUAL DEFIANT
RARITY: RARE
SET: AIR STRIKE

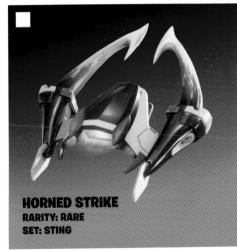

HORNED STRIKE
RARITY: RARE
SET: STING

JUNK BUCKET
RARITY: EPIC
SET: STORM SCAVENGER

MASTER MIX
RARITY: EPIC
SET: TWIN TURNTABLES

NITE FLIGHT
RARITY: RARE
SET: DREAMY DAYS

PIXEL PILOT
RARITY: RARE
SET: SPACE EXPLORERS

RIFT RIDER
RARITY: RARE
SET: DRIFT

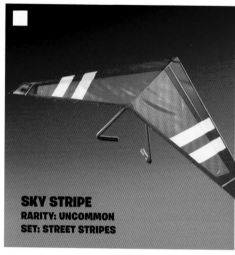

SKY STRIPE
RARITY: UNCOMMON
SET: STREET STRIPES

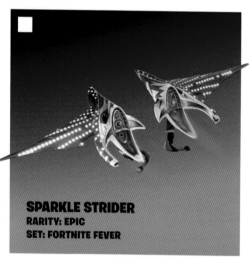

SPARKLE STRIDER
RARITY: EPIC
SET: FORTNITE FEVER

SPRAY SAIL
RARITY: RARE
SET: AEROSOL ASSASSINS

STEELWING
RARITY: LEGENDARY
SET: FORT KNIGHTS

STUNT CYCLE
RARITY: RARE
SET: RPM

X
RARITY: COMMON

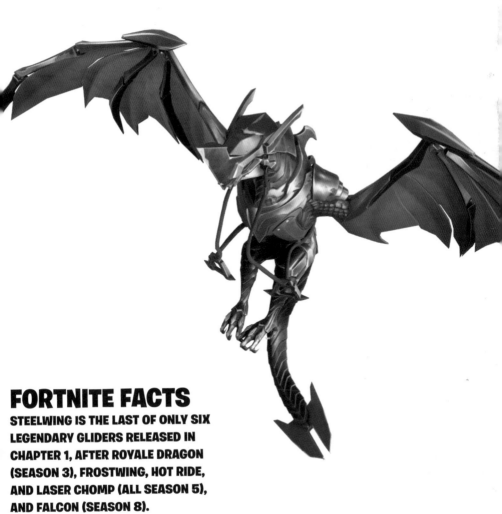

FORTNITE FACTS
STEELWING IS THE LAST OF ONLY SIX LEGENDARY GLIDERS RELEASED IN CHAPTER 1, AFTER ROYALE DRAGON (SEASON 3), FROSTWING, HOT RIDE, AND LASER CHOMP (ALL SEASON 5), AND FALCON (SEASON 8).

BEAT DROP
RARITY: RARE
SET: TWIN TURNTABLES

CELESTIAL
RARITY: RARE

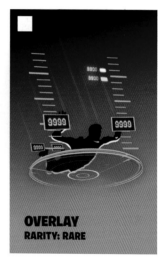

OVERLAY
RARITY: RARE

POPCORN
RARITY: RARE

RIFT LIGHTNING
RARITY: RARE
SET: DRIFT

FORTNITE FACTS

ONE OF THE MOST EYE-CATCHING CONTRAILS IN FORTNITE, OVERLAY WILL STREAM A TRAIL OF COMPUTERIZED NUMBERS BEHIND YOU AS YOU DROP IN.

BLOWING BUBBLES
RARITY: RARE

BREAKNECK
RARITY: EPIC

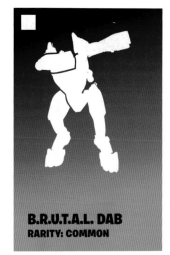

B.R.U.T.A.L. DAB
RARITY: COMMON

BURPEE
RARITY: UNCOMMON

DABSTAND
RARITY: UNCOMMON

FEATHERWEIGHT
RARITY: UNCOMMON

FULL TILT
RARITY: RARE

GO HOME!
RARITY: UNCOMMON

HANG ON
RARITY: UNCOMMON

INFECTIOUS
RARITY: RARE

JAYWALKING
RARITY: RARE

JITTERBUG
RARITY: RARE

LEVITATE
RARITY: LEGENDARY
SET: OVERSEER

LLAMA CONGA
RARITY: RARE

MOON BOUNCE
RARITY: RARE

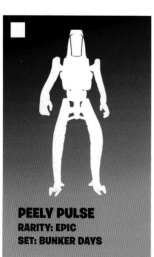

PEELY PULSE
RARITY: EPIC
SET: BUNKER DAYS

PIZZA PARTY
RARITY: UNCOMMON
SET: PIZZA PIT

POOF
RARITY: UNCOMMON

RAGE QUIT
RARITY: UNCOMMON

STATUESQUE
RARITY: UNCOMMON

STRIDE
RARITY: RARE

SUGAR RUSH
RARITY: RARE

TACO TIME
RARITY: RARE
SET: THE LEFTOVERS

TEAM BURGER
RARITY: UNCOMMON
SET: THE LEFTOVERS

TEAM SPACE
RARITY: UNCOMMON
SET: UFO

TEAM TOMATO
RARITY: UNCOMMON
SET: THE LEFTOVERS

TRA LA LA
RARITY: UNCOMMON

TSSSSS
RARITY: RARE

VERY SNEAKY
RARITY: RARE

VIBIN'
RARITY: RARE

WELCOME!
RARITY: UNCOMMON

WHERE IS MATT?
RARITY: RARE

WINDMILL FLOSS
RARITY: RARE

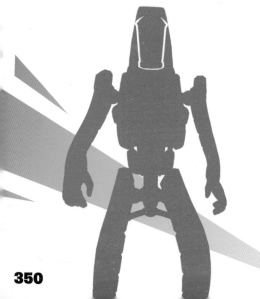

FORTNITE FACTS
**PEELY PULSE IS THE BUILT-IN EMOTE
THAT COMES WITH THE P-1000 OUTFIT
AND COULD BE OBTAINED THROUGH
THE P-1000 CHALLENGE PACK.**